A BORDER BAIRN

LAVINIA DERWENT

A Border Bairn

Illustrated by Elizabeth Haines

Arrow Books

Also in Arrow by Lavinia Derwent

A Breath of Border Air
God Bless the Borders!
Lady of the Manse

Arrow Books Limited
62-65 Chandos Place, London WC2N 4NW

An imprint of Century Hutchinson Ltd

London Melbourne Sydney Auckland
Johannesburg and agencies throughout
the world

First published by Hutchinson 1979
Arrow edition 1980
Reprinted 1986

Printed and bound in Great Britain by
Anchor Brendon Limited, Tiptree, Essex

ISBN 0 09 922200 0

In memory of Overton Bush

Contents

1. There is a Happy Land

When I was very young the past seemed a long way off. I used to talk to Jessie about the olden days. Meaning last week.

'Havers, lassie! Wait till ye're as auld as me.'

I have waited, and true enough, the past seems nearer. Like yesterday.

I can see it all as plainly as if I were there in the farmhouse kitchen in the Cheviots, sitting on the rug in the lamplight with the big black kettle spitting on the swey and the sheep-dip calendar hanging on the wall. *When Did You Last See Your Father?*

The noise I hear is the clatter of Jessie's clogs on the stone kitchen floor, the rattle of her milking-pail and the piercing whistle outside from Jock-the-herd calling his collies to heel. I smell the fragrance of appleringie growing in the front garden amongst the tangle of flowers and weeds, and feel the sting of nettles on my bare legs as I go stravaiging through the woods.

I am there and it is all happening.

Sometimes the picture blurs and in the fading light I begin to wonder. Was it really like that or am I making it up, filling in the gaps with imagination? Memory can play strange tricks. Yet the mind's eye often produces a truthful picture. I have been back to the old homestead and looked at it face-to-face. It was real enough, but no more real than when I see it from a far distance. Long sight is sometimes better than short.

Half-forgotten visions often sharpen into focus, and I am suddenly reminded of someone who dominated my young life for many a year. The strange thing was I never met him in the flesh though he lived with us and was as much part of the household as the grandfather clock in the hall. I could see the clock clearly enough but I never set eyes on the mysterious stranger who caused such havoc about the place.

I used to puzzle my head about him, wondering what he looked like and where he hid himself. In the garret, maybe, though I never saw him when I was imprisoned there for my misdeeds. In the dark press we called the glory-hole, or even under the floorboards? Sometimes I heard creakings at dead of night. Could they be caused by the invisible man's footsteps?

Jessie was the one who knew him best, and not a good word had she to say for him. According to her he was a bad rascal. 'Maister Naebody' she called him. A nasty nuisance who deserved a good skelping; and Jessie's skelps were not soon forgotten.

I had a sneaking sympathy for Mr Nobody in spite of his wicked ways, for were not his habits much the same as mine? Mr Nobody broke windows, knocked the teapot off the table, stopped the clock, spilt ink on the floor, hid keys and lost the scissors. A clumsy creature with no rummle-gumption. Jessie's word for common sense. She was full of it.

'Ye'll no' hae seen the poker onywhere?' she would say to me accusingly.

'Me? No, I've not.'

'A'weel, somebody's gane an' lost it. It'll be that Maister Naebody at his tricks again, the bad rascal.'

Jessie herself was perfect in every way. Staunch and true, as straight as a die, her word was her bond. Every job she tackled was done with the utmost thoroughness, from scrubbing the kitchen floor to extracting a skelf from a sore thumb. She could milk cows, stook corn, spread dung, patch breeks, bake scones, kirn butter; and, if the occasion arose, lay out a dead body. 'The back's aye made for the burden' was one of her sayings, and certainly hers was often overloaded.

With such an example to follow it was disappointing that I did now grow up more perfect myself, instead of copying Maister Naebody. But Jessie's goal was far beyond my reach. She saw everything in black and white; good or bad, no half measures. The good went to heaven and the bad to hell. There was no doubt in which direction I was aiming.

The minister often spoke about sins when he was preaching in the village kirk on the Sabbath day. Transgressions, he called them. What a wicked lot we were, straying from the paths of righteousness, thinking evil thoughts and doing bad deeds. We had all erred – that was another of his Sunday words – in the sight of the Lord, and broken all the commandments. The Thou Shalt Nots. Unless we repented and humbly begged for mercy we would be cast into outer darkness and end our days in the fiery furnace. All except His Reverence, of course. He was above all that and never transgressed. At least, not on Sundays.

At the Sunday School we had to learn the Shorter Catechism off by heart. Gabble-gabble-gabble. If there was a longer one, we were fortunate not to come across it. What a driech treatise it was, full of obscure ramblings.

'Man's chief end is to glorify God and enjoy Him for ever.'

'What does it mean?' I once asked Big Bob, who was sitting beside me on the hard pew, staring into space and fingering the catapult in his pocket for consolation.

'I've nae idea,' he said, looking startled. 'It's just blethers.'

It seemed impossible for a sinner like myself to pass the qualifying exam that would let me in through the pearly gates; so, as I was on the road to hell anyway, why bother to be good? I might as well tell lies, break crockery, kick the cat, plunk from the school, and enjoy my transgressions. But there was something that held me back. Could it be that strange inward thing the minister called conscience? Or maybe it was Jessie's upright example.

'Is there nothing you can't do, Jessie?' I once asked her.

'Ay,' she said with a straight face. 'I canna pit ma big tae in ma mooth.'

Even to hear her talk was a treat, she had such a rich store of expressive words. Sometimes she spoke to Blackie, the kitchen cat, sitting yawning on the rug.

'Daursay! what are ye gantin' for? Stir your stumps an' get oot ma road.'

She never had to tell me to stir my stumps for I was always on the go. On the randan, like a peerie-top, Jessie said. But I would sit still long enough on my stool in the byre if I could coax her to tell one of her stories while she was milking the kye. About a cushy-doo, maybe, or a wee centipede called Meggy-Mony-Feet.

I lived in a world of double-talk. English as it was spoken at the Grammar School and broad Border as spoken by the hinds who worked in the fields. With a sprinkling of Geordie dialect from the Sassenachs who lived beyond the Carter Bar. Bitter enemies in the days when we harried each others' nests; now friendly neighbours who came to pay peaceful visits unarmed with battleaxes. I could even master a few French phrases now that I was in the Higher Grade. The less said about Latin the better.

But amongst all the voices from the past it is Jessie's I hear most often, muffled as she dug her head into the cow's side. 'A'weel, ance upon a time there was a wee weasel ca'd Wullie Whitterick . . . '

Though the farm was so far removed from human contact it had the great charm of being surrounded on all sides by the beauties of Nature. 'The Borders is beautiful' was a common saying. Yet I once heard a cottage wife sigh in the depths of boredom: 'Eh whowh! I'm fair fed up wi' scenery. Day in, day oot. Naethin' but scenery.'

For my part I never grew tired of gazing at the Cheviots or at the triple-peaked Eildon Hills where King Arthur and his knights lay slumbering, awaiting the call that would one day release them from 'the bondage of enchantment'. It was the great Wizard, Michael Scott, who had cleft the hills in twain, merely by saying some magic words. I often wondered what they could be. We were studying Sir Walter Scott's *Lay of the Last Minstrel* at school. *He* knew the answer.

> And, Warrior, I would say to thee
> The words that cleft Eildon hills in three
> And bridled the Tweed with a curb of stone,
> But to speak them were a deadly sin,
> And for having but thought them my heart within
> A treble penance must be done.

So Sir Walter kept the secret to himself and I never found out. Otherwise I might have tried the magic on our own hill at home.

Some of Jessie's words were difficult to translate into plain English, but they were so expressive that their meaning was easily guessed. A chatterbox was a bletherskite, a tell-tale a clype, a round-shouldered person was humphy-backit, a throat was a thrapple, a turkey-cock a bubblyjock, upside-down was tapsulteerie, and dumfoonert meant astonished. It was far better fun than a dead language like Latin.

There was another language. Bad language. But strangely enough I never heard much of it around the farm. Maybe the hinds curbed their tongues in my presence, and the most I heard the herd say when aggravated by a straying sheep was: 'Damned eediot!' And on occasions he would call me a wee deevil, which I took to be a form of endearment.

In the Sunday School we sniggered at rude words in the bible. Belly, for example, and fornication, which we guessed was something dirty though we were not sure what. The minister was forever talking about hell and damnation, but he had been specially chosen by the Almighty and could say what he liked. As for hidden parts of the anatomy, we never mentioned them at all, and as far as I knew they had no names, not even Latin ones.

It was always to Jessie and the farmworkers I turned rather than to the immediate members of my family who seemed too engrossed in their own affairs to bother about mine. Perhaps I am doing them an injustice. Who was I, anyway? Only an in-between. Father and Mother were kind enough, providing me with what they considered the necessities of life. Food, clothing, a roof over my head. My elder brother and sister were naturally more important, being the first son and daughter. A fourth child was already toddling around on unsteady feet, and a fifth was expected, though as yet I could see no visible signs of it. So there was nothing special about me.

Except to myself. Young or old, we all crave recognition. 'Look at me! Listen to me! Talk to me! I am somebody! Not merely a mouth to be fed and a body to be clothed. I am not an also-ran. I am a person in my own right.'

Jessie noticed me, at least, now and again, for which I was truly grateful. So did her brother, the shepherd, who accepted me more or less as one of his flock. A yowe or a gimmer, a stirk or a stot. Or maybe just a damned eediot. 'Man-lassie', he called me.

There was always plenty for me to notice in the things around me. The self-sufficiency of Nature never failed to amaze me. There was surely a touch of Michael Scott's wizardry in the way a fragile snowdrop forced its way through the frozen ground or a crocus suddenly appeared from nowhere. I had a great curiosity to see how things grew, to listen to the earth and hear seeds bursting into life, but though I watched and listened I could never notice any movement. The flowers seemed to wait till my back was turned before thrusting their way through the ground.

It was the same with my baby brother who suddenly stood on his feet and began to stagger around by himself. The day before he had been a helpless child, unable to fend for himself and having to be carried everywhere. I, too, was shooting up like the snowdrops, though I could not feel myself growing. Yet I was constantly needing larger sizes in shoes and the hems of my frocks let down.

The first foreign visitors I ever saw were the swallows who flew all the way from Africa to nest under the eaves of our sheds. I wondered how on earth they had found their way from all that distance. Nature was full of unexplained mysteries, and who could give the answer? God, who had made all creatures great and small.

Sometimes in spring I went into the nearby wood and listened to all the sounds around me. Restless exciting sounds like those of an orchestra tuning up. The cawing of the rooks mixing with the melody of other birdsongs, the soughing of the wind, the hum of insects scurrying secretly in the undergrowth, the yelp of a fox in the distance, and Jock shouting to his sheepdogs. 'Doon, Jess! 'Way by, Jed!'

If I kept still enough I could watch the birds building their nests, astonished at their energy and ingenuity. The results were always perfect, though the raw materials at their command were so simple. Anything they could carry in their beaks was grist to them. Wisps of wool, hair, straw, mud, moss, feathers, rabbits' fur, spiders' webs. There was never anything slapdash or higgledy-piggledy about their home-made houses. Each bird was his own architect, fashioning his nest to suit his own special needs.

> A wee bit biggin', neatly made
> To keep ma bairnies in the shade . . .

Some of the nests were concealed in the hedges. Others under eaves, in tree trunks, rusty pails, discarded wheelbarrows, or in the bole of a tree. Pheasants and partridges were experts at camouflage, making simple bields on the ground amongst heather and bracken, carefully covering them with dead leaves or grass before flying off to forage for food.

It was a sin, I had been told, to rob a bird's nest. The mother would come flying after me and peck my eyes out.

> The robin and the lintie,
> The laverock and the wren,
> Them that herries their nests
> Will never thrive again.

It was exciting enough just to find a nest, perhaps a hedge-sparrow's, which I could watch till the fledgelings hatched out and flew away to begin another cycle of life on their own.

I began to puzzle, as young folk will, about the eternal verities of life. Everything must have been put on earth for a purpose, from the moles under the ground to the eagles in the sky. It was the same, I supposed, with human beings, though as yet I had not discovered my own purpose on earth, but there must be some reason for my existence, apart from just being a nuisance to everybody.

There were so few human beings around me that I was able to study each one individually with such intensity that I came to know every wrinkle on the hinds' faces and each bristle on their cheeks. The herd had shaggy eyebrows that shot up and down, and Father had a dimple in his chin.

My father was a good-looking man, I thought, and never handsomer than when he wore his straw hat in summer. The straw basher. He put it on at a rakish angle and looked quite the gentleman, according to Jessie. But anything he wore, even his night-shirt, seemed to suit him, giving proof to another Border saying: 'A weel-faured face sets a dishcloot.'

When I saw a strange face at the door, even if it was only a packman's, it was like having a new book to read, though such treats were few and far between. A young gallant straying from the hunt might ride by or a salesman arrive in a motor car, trying to talk the Boss into ordering some farm accessory. And once the Maiden Ladies who were real gentry, related to the laird himself at the Big Hoose, drove up in their dog-cart and deigned to come in for a cup of tea.

Luckily for us, Bella at the Post Office, acting as our go-between, had rung up to give us advance warning. The best china and the lace-edged tablecloth were set out in readiness, and a batch of pancakes and scones – daintier than usual – had been hurriedly baked.

The visit of the high-bred Maiden Ladies, with their spotted veils, their silks and frills, their gold pendants, bangles, brooches and rings – and above all their refined conversation – kept me going long after they had driven away in their buggy down the bumpy farm road, leaving a waft of eau de Cologne behind. They were made of finer stuff, yet I liked the tramps best. The criss-cross lines on their weatherbeaten faces seemed to tell more adventurous tales than those of the papier-poudréd Ladies.

The gaun-aboot bodies, as Jessie called the tramps, were

adepts at mooching, and never refused any cast-off especially if it could be worn on their extremities. Carpet slippers, wellington boots, plimsolls, clogs, leggings, spats, elastic-sided boots. Everything was welcome. They themselves never discarded any of their gear no matter how down-at-heel. Even if the soles were hanging off they clung to their old bauchles, wrapping them up in newspapers in the belief that they would come in handy some day.

'They'll kep a catch,' was their way of expressing it.

An old crone called Nellie Naebody was one of our regulars. When I asked her if she was related to the mysterious Maister Naebody who lived in our house she said, 'Ay, he's ma faither.' But she had a glint in her eye as she spoke, and I knew from Jessie that she was not quite right in the head, apart from being over-fond of the bottle. I liked to watch her puffing at her clay pipe. Being toothless, she could suck in her cheeks and contort her face as if it was made of india-rubber.

If we were left on our own Nellie would sidle closer to me so that she could whisper confidentially in my ear, as if she had an important secret to impart. Usually it was only a request for clothing.

'A pair o' drawers or an auld semmit. Onything'll do.'

If I came back with a torn blazer instead, discarded by my elder brother, or with a moth-eaten fur tippet, she accepted them gratefully and put them on there and then.

'The verra dab! Jings! this is ma lucky day. Here's a ha'penny left in the pooch.'

One day when we were sitting alone on the bench outside the kitchen door Nellie gave me a nudge and whispered: 'What aboot gettin' me a drap oot the bottle? Just a moothfou', for ma asthma.' She gave a convincing wheeze. 'Ye can easy manage it, a clever lass like you. Mum's the word.'

Flattery of any kind always went to my head, so off I set on my furtive mission, not too sure how much a wee drap was or if I could escape the watchful eyes of the rest of the household. At least I knew where my father kept his secret bottle. In the parlour cabinet.

Luckily the key was in the lock, but first I had to look for a container of some kind into which I could decant the whisky. The best I could find after a hurried search was a small cascara bottle with some of the medicine still in the bottom. There was no time to wash it out so I just left it there.

Filling the small bottle from the big one was a tricky job, requiring great concentration and a steady hand. Mine was shaky through fear of being discovered. Blackie, the kitchen cat, came through and lapped up the overflow that trickled on to the carpet, than gave a strange miaow as she licked her lips. She looked up at me with a puzzled expression as if asking for an explanation, but I had problems of my own.

At last the deed was done. I managed to dodge Jessie and bore the cascara bottle in triumph out to Nellie who was waiting impatiently for my return.

'That's the stuff!' said she, seizing the bottle and draining its contents to the last drop, medicine and all. Then she belched blissfully, wiped her mouth on her ragged sleeve and gave me a toothless grin. 'Clever lass! Ye'll get your reward in heaven.'

But not on earth. There was a great to-do when Father found out that someone had been tampering with his whisky bottle. Who was the culprit?

'Maister Naebody,' said Jessie, pursing her lips. 'The bad rascal.'

I never confessed, and felt guilty about it for a while, but at least Nellie went down the road singing.

I sometimes sang myself but only if I was out of earshot of other folk. On the hill was a safe place, in the old keep which was my favourite sanctuary, with only the whaups and the shilfies to hear. I sang anything that came into my head. Miss Thing, the music-teacher at the Grammar School, was obsessed with part-songs. 'Who is Sylvia? What is she?' We were not allowed to bawl as we had done at the village school when Auld Baldy-Heid used to teach us 'Come, follow', or 'Oh, who will o'er the downs so free?'

Miss Thing conducted us with a long cane and rapped us over the head if we strayed from the tune. We had to keep thinking about breath-control, and beats in the bar. She sorted us all out into sopranos, contraltos, tenors and basses, with some of the boys – known as the grunters – being neither one thing nor the other. I would have liked to join them, but I had been classed as a soprano and often had to push my voice up to impossible heights, always terrified I would end up in a skirl.

Out on the hill it did not matter. I could be a grunter if I liked. The main thing was to make a joyful sound. And in spite of the many sad thoughts of youth it was surprising how often happiness had a habit of breaking through. The only way of expressing it was by singing. Not about Sylvia and her swains. Rollicking songs which Father sometimes sang at local concerts. 'Paddy McGinty's Goat', 'The Bonnie Bonnie Hoose o' Airlie', and 'The Lum Hat Wantin' a Croon'.

Sometimes for a change I sang one of the children's hymns we were taught in the Sunday School about the happy land that is far away. But as I sat singing it on the crumbling castle wall, I knew that the hymn was wrong. The happy land was not far away. It was here in the Borders.

2. Milestones

The first recognition I ever received was when I had my name printed in the local paper. The *Jedburgh Gazette*, known locally as the 'Jethart Squeaker'. For winning second prize in the egg-and-spoon race at the Sunday School sports.

It would have been better if I had been first, but I was quite pleased to be mentioned at all. There was my name for all to see, alongside an item on foot-and-mouth disease and underneath a blurred photograph of the laird. He, too, had been at the sports, though not competing against me, but he did present me with my prize. A silver sixpence. The first prize, won by a lassie from over the Border, was a shilling. Such wealth.

Not that the money mattered; it was the fact that I had done something worth recording. Up till then fame had never been my spur. I had determined that if ever any of my writings were published I would sign them 'Anon', like the poet in my schoolbook. Not only so that none could shower me with fulsome flattery, but chiefly that they should not scoff.

'Fancy her writing stuff like that! Set her up!'

For, of course, no home-brewed talent could be worth anything.

'Her! *She* canna be famous. I went to the schule wi' her.'

It was always the stranger, the unknown quantity, who was worthy of praise.

But when I appeared in the Squeaker I threw all scruples to the wind.

'See, Jock, look!' I cried, running out to the shepherd with the crumpled newspaper in my hand. 'There's my name!'

'Where? Haud on till I find ma specs.'

Jock fumbled in his pooch and finally brought out the family spectacles shared in turn with his sisters Jessie and Joo-anne. 'Mexty me! so it is. Weel done, you!'

It was a great moment of triumph for me, compensating for all the hard training I had put in, running round the farmyard with a nest egg balanced on an old teaspoon. I could never find anyone to compete against me – Jessie had better things to do than run races – nor could I always lay my hands on a nest egg. So sometimes I used a real one, which made the operation a great deal trickier, often ending with the egg smashed to smithereens and Jessie raging, 'Ye're a wastrif article, so ye are. Think o' a' the stervin' Chinese.'

When Jessie called me an article I knew I had reached rock bottom. But even she was impressed when I drew her attention to the item in the paper, though she could not see it properly without her spectacles. I read it out to her – twice – in case she missed anything.

'Weel, fancy that!'

It was nothing much to say but I knew she was pleased. I was no longer just an article.

Then she astounded me with her next statement.

'It's no' the first time ye've been in the Squeaker.'

'Me?'

'Ay, you! Ye were in when ye were hatched.'

'When was I hatched?'

'Hoots! when ye were born. A'body gets into the paper when they're hatched, matched or dispatched. I've been in masel'.'

I tried to imagine Jessie hatching from an egg, cracking her way out through the shell and struggling to her feet to tie on a coarse apron. A brat, she called it. She would set about at once to stir the porridge or milk the cows. I could not visualise an interim period when she played with a skipping rope or made daisy-chains.

'When were you hatched, Jessie?'

'Mind your ain business, an' dinna let the Squeaker gang to your heid.'

But it did, of course.

I had forgotten all about Anon and my desire to hide my light under a bushel. With the inconsistency of youth I changed direction like a weathercock. My likes and dislikes were never too rigid to alter. One moment I would fancy I disliked the taste of tomatoes. The next I would see someone else eating them with such relish that I decided to follow suit. They were good; I liked tomatoes! The same with my Sunday hat. I hated the sight of it till someone praised it, after which it was seldom off my head.

I had an off-on relationship, by the same token, with the cottage wives. One day I decided never to speak to Mrs Thing again. Never-ever! She had deliberately, I felt sure, shaken her rug in my face as I passed on the way to school. So that was the end of her.

The very next day she was at her door calling out to me, 'Hi, lassie, wad ye do an obleegement for me? I'm needin' a new scrubbin'-brush. Could I bother ye to buy me ane in the toon?'

'No bother,' I agreed readily, pleased that she had credited me with enough gumption to undertake such a mission. When she handed me the money and said, 'Ye can keep the change,' her stock rose higher. She was nice, Mrs Thing.

But it was even nicer finding fame in the local paper, and not merely in the district, for the Squeaker was posted overseas to exiled Borderers hungry for home news. Cousins and uncles who had emigrated to Canada and Australia. Imagine them reading about me in the Rocky Mountains or New South Wales.

I could picture them eagerly opening the paper, scanning every item and saying when they saw my name, 'Ay! that'll be her frae Overton Bush. The Buss! A wee smout o' a lass wi' red hair. I kent her faither an' mither. Nice folk. Ye got a grand spread in their fermhoose. Sic teas! Toddie-scones an' sponge-cake. Melted in the mooth.'

The great thing about the Squeaker was that no detail was left out. Every name was mentioned, down to who brewed the tea at a whist drive, who won the booby prize and who said a few well-chosen words in the vote of thanks. 'Mr Tom Scott of the Mains made some witty remarks. (Applause).'

Never mind the outside world. The *Scotsman* could take care of revolutions, assassinations and general elections. What we wanted to read about was a roup at a neighbouring farm (a roup being a sale), that there had been an accident in the High Street (two bicycles bumped together: one wheel buckled), that the kirk soirée had been a resounding success, the laird was laid low with sciatica, a runaway bull had been rounded up at Southdean, and Mrs Rutherford's washing had been stolen from the line (vagrants suspected).

If there was a shortage of happenings the gap was sometimes filled by the insertion of a starting headline: OUTBREAK OF SMALLPOX, with a statement underneath to the effect that 'There have been no cases of smallpox in the district lately'. It was a sure way of riveting the reader's attention.

I liked the Fifty Years Ago column where I might come across a familiar name. Maybe my Granny's. 'Perfect attendance at the Sunday School.' Or an item about good Queen Victoria. 'Her Gracious Majesty has arrived safely at Balmoral. May the sun shine on Her.' Surely it would never dare to rain.

Sometimes there were touching little poems in the dispatched column. In Memoriam, written no doubt by Anon.

> A year ago on this sad day
> The Lord called Agnes Scott away.
> The pearly gates were opened wide
> And angels welcomed her inside.

More cheerful items could be found amongst the court cases. 'A labourer of no fixed abode was apprehended after attempting to climb the clock tower. He pleaded that he was short-sighted and wanted to see the time, but PC Brown believed the man had been imbibing strong drink. Thirty days.'

What a lot one could learn from the Jethart Squeaker. That there would be a retiring collection next Sunday for the schemes of the church, that there was to be a sale of damaged goods in a shop in Jedburgh (terrible bargains), that a garden fête would be opened by Lady Somebody at Edgerston House (entrance 1/-, tea thrown in), that a part-time woman was wanted in a farmhouse (must be strong, willing and a good milker), that a budgie had been lost, stolen or strayed (answers to the name of Bobby and can whistle 'Happy Birthday to You'. Reward).

Now that I had appeared in it myself I held the local paper in even higher esteem and tried to prevent Jessie from lining the dresser drawer with it.

'Stop! Wait till I've cut out the bit about me.'

'Ye're a conceited article,' she sniffed; but all the same she handed me the scissors and I kept the cutting till it became too frayed to read. By that time, in any case, I had gone on to higher things. *First* prize in the sack race. But the thrill was never the same again.

Earlier in my life, while I was still at the village school, I passed another milestone on the day I was promoted to a pen, a sure sign that I was no longer a backward infant.

Auld Baldy-Heid, the teacher, came round with a huge earthenware bottle of blue-black ink and poured some into the little inkwell on my desk. Then he presented me with a new pen and a sheet of blotting-paper, warning me at the same time not to make a mess. What he actually said was, 'You'd better not make a slaister.' A slaister being something even messier than a mess.

He might have saved his breath. In next to no time I succeeded in making the biggest slaister possible. It was quite easy. With all that ink at my disposal there were soon stains on my fingers, smudges on my face, blots on my copybook, and the pen itself was needing a new nib.

The copybook had uplifting proverbs on the top of each page in perfect calligraphy which I was supposed to copy in the same flawless style. 'Waste not want not.' 'A rolling stone gathers no moss.' 'He who hesitates is lost.' And so on. I felt there ought to have been another one, specially for me. 'Thou shalt not slaister thy copybook.'

Being newfangled at the job I was constantly dipping the pen too far into the inkwell and pressing too hard on the nib, with the result that it splayed out and spluttered ink in all directions. Without even trying I scored a bull's-eye on Big Bob who was so enraged when a blob of ink landed on his nose that he retaliated there and then by seizing my pigtails and dipping the ends in his own inkwell.

If I had been in a mess before I was in a real slaister by now.

Still, I felt quite proud of my battle-stains as I wended my way home that day. Anyone could tell just by looking at me that I was on my way up in the world. Anyone except Jock-the-herd whom I met on the farm road and who never noticed anything unless it was connected with sheep. He played into my hands by asking, 'Man-lassie, are ye needin' ony pencils sherpened?'

'No, thanks. I'm in pens now,' I said haughtily.

All the same I would miss the ministrations of my chief pencil-sharpener. For years Jock had done the deed for me with a fearsome-looking jack-knife which he took out from the depths of his pocket. It had several blades of varying sizes and was used for a multitude of purposes. Howking turnips out of the field, cutting off lengths of bindertwine, clipping tufts of wool from a sheep's back. Even, as I discovered to my horror, cutting their throats when they had to be killed. Gouging tobacco from his pipe, and, of course, sharpening my 'keelies', as he sometimes called them.

As time went by there were occasions when I wished I was back in the old days when I could rub out my pencilled mistakes. Not so easy to erase wrong answers penned in blotchy ink. Jock agreed with me. 'Man-lassie, when I was at the schule it was slate pencils. Awfu' handy. Ye could just wipe oot the mistakes wi' your sleeve.'

Never will I forget the day we were set to write an essay. My Favourite Holiday. Most of the class had never been on holiday at all, except Chrissie Scott who was always boasting about visiting M'Auntie in Hawick. All very well for her. The rest of us dipped our pens despairingly into our inkwells and dredged our brains for inspiration. Mine came when I suddenly decided the essay need not be true, and embarked on a long saga about spending a week in London. The idea! London!

What a week it was! I missed nothing. I sailed on the Thames, visited the Houses of Parliament, fed the pigeons in Trafalgar Square, and was about to have tea in Buckingham Palace when my pen ran dry. My inkwell was empty.

I put up my hand to attract the teacher's attention. On such occasions Auld Baldy-Heid, who normally had eyes in the back of his head, seemed to have lost his sight. Or, as on this particular day, had hidden himself behind the *Scotsman* and refused to emerge. The thing to do in such a situation was to snap one's fingers so that he could hear the noise and look up. But snapping my fingers was not one of my accomplishments. Try as I would I could never make even the feeblest sound, so I prevailed upon Big Bob, who could snap like a thunderclap, to do the deed for me.

'Yes?' said Auld Baldy-Heid, reluctantly looking up. I could see from his expression that he meant 'No!'

'Please s-sir, I've r-run out of ink.'

A black frown from the master. 'Again!' he said in an irritated voice. 'What do you do with it, woman? Drink it?'

'N-no, sir.'

Auld Baldy-Heid rustled his newspaper. 'You can use your pencil,' he said sharply and went back to his reading.

'Please s-sir, I've l-lost it.' Which was not quite true. I had given it away to Wee Maggie who was still working painfully at her pothooks. 'What'll I do, sir?' It would be a pity not to have tea in Buckingham Palace for want of a drop of ink.

More impatient rustlings of the *Scotsman*. Then, 'Go and help yourself,' said Auld Baldy-Heid gruffly. 'And don't . . .' The rest of the sentence was muffled but it was not difficult to guess he was warning me not to make a slaister.

It was a moment of triumph for me, going out in front of the class to lift down the heavy jar from the shelf, the envy of all eyes, particularly Big Bob's. No one else had ever been granted such a privilege.

'See me!' I thought proudly. 'Auld Baldy-Heid trusts me. I'll make a good job of it.'

I did.

If only the jar had not been so heavy all would have gone well. It was an awkward job unscrewing the stopper and tipping the bottle at the right angle so that the ink would trickle rather than gush into the small inkwell. The overflow ran down my desk and drip-dropped on to the floor like a waterfall.

'Slaister!' hissed Big Bob, gloating at my mishap. 'You'll catch it!' At which point the worst happened. Somehow or other the heavy jar slipped through my fingers and crashed to the floor, shattering into a hundred fragments.

Before horror overtook me, I spared a sympathetic thought for one of our servant-lasses, a clumsy creature nicknamed the Carthorse, who was for ever dropping teapots and breaking jugs. 'It just fell oot ma hand,' was her constant excuse.

As I stared at the rivulets of ink running across the floor like blue-black streams, I shared some of her feelings. Blacker than the ink was Auld Baldy-Heid's frown as he flung aside his newspaper and sprang at me like a tiger on its prey.

'You stupid idiot!'

He got no further. I was saved by a knock on the school-room door, followed by the entrance of the minister arriving on one of his periodic visits to 'give us our religion'.

He saw the mess on the floor, of course. How could he help it since he stepped into one of the puddles and splashed ink on to his socks? Black, fortunately.

'Just a small accident,' said the master with a false smile on his face; but out of the corner of his mouth he hissed at me, 'You'll stay behind tonight, my lady!'

My lady knew this was equivalent to the death sentence. We were all accustomed to being punished by the strap. Short, sharp, and soon over. If it did us no good it did us no harm. Staying behind meant being left alone at the mercy of Auld Baldy-Heid who used this form of punishment only in the most stringent cases, since he was always in a hurry to get rid of the lot of us and go home to the schoolhouse for his tea. I had no idea what form of torment he had up his sleeve. It had never happened to me before, so my imagination ran riot and I saw myself strung up from the ceiling, tortured with red-hot pokers, my head scalped and my eyes gouged out. Would I ever live to tell the tale?

When the minister gave out a hymn I found it difficult to join in the singing of 'I'm a little pilgrim' accompanied on the piano by Auld Baldy-Heid playing with one finger. Between verses I tried to mop up some of the ink with my blotting-paper and any I could borrow from my classmates. Even Big Bob was sympathetic enough to lend me his. By the time His Reverence had given us his blessing most of the mess had dried up though one blotch remained never to be erased, a permanent mark of my shame. Perhaps it is there to this day.

My visit to Buckingham Palace never took place, for as soon as the minister left Auld Baldy-Heid decided to turn his attention to sums. Mental arithmetic. Not another word about spilt ink. This was ominous in itself, and for the rest of the day the sword of Damocles dangled over my head and I wondered if I ought to make my will, not that I had anything much to leave.

Mental arithmetic was not my strong point. The master rapped out the numbers at top speed. I tried to catch them and add them up as they flew through the air. Five, seven, twelve, sixteen, twenty-two, thirty-eight . . . It was hopeless trying to reach the right answer. Fortunately I was not the only defaulter and in the end Auld Baldy-Heid gave up in exasperation.

'You're a lot of dolts. Stupid idiots! I'll write the sums on the blackboard.'

As the dreadful day went by we pursued the uneven tenor of our ways, jumping from sums to history – Bruce and the spider – and from there to poetry.

> Up from the meadows rich with corn,
> Clear on a cool September morn,
> The something spires of Brunswick stand . . .

Something was a great word if mumbled in the right way and if the teacher was not listening too intently. We could get away with murder, but not in my case with staying behind, though I kept hoping against hope that my executioner might forget. Not Auld Baldy-Heid.

When the lucky ones rushed away like convicts escaping from prison, some pausing long enough to throw me a backward glance of pity, I was left in limbo, wondering if I would ever see any of them again. Auld Baldy-Heid was rubbing out the sums from the blackboard and replacing them with a warning sentence. 'Be sure your sins will find you out.'

'Copy that in your best writing, over and over again,' he said sternly. 'I'll be back.' With that he went away round to the schoolhouse for his tea, locking the door behind him.

It was not the copying that worried me. It was the 'I'll be back'. With what weapons of torture? Thumbscrews, a sharp knife, maybe even a gun?

It was strange sitting alone in the empty classroom with no shuffling feet to be heard. No sniffles, giggles or groans. I would have welcomed even Big Bob, the bully, tugging at my hair or Wee Maggie whispering, 'Could you lend me a penthil, pleathe? I've lotht mine.' I could only plough on, filling page after page of my copybook. At least I had plenty of ink.

Be sure your sins will find you out. I was certain by now.

Having served so many sentences of solitary confinement in the garret at home, I was accustomed to being imprisoned; but that was a familiar gaol with plenty of distractions. An old rocking-horse to ride, bound volumes of the *Quiver* to read, a chest full of discarded finery to rummage through, a rickety washstand to climb on when I wanted to push up the skylight window and peer down at the free world. Here I was forced to sit in one place and await my fate.

The shades of night were falling so fast that I could scarcely see my copybook. The blackboard creaked and shadowy figures lurked in every corner. By now I was writing the sentence mechanically and getting it all fankled. Be sin your sures will out you find.

It was the *Scotsman* that saved me. Auld Baldy-Heid, having forgotten all about me and my sins, remembered he had left his paper in the schoolroom and came round to fetch it. Otherwise I might have spent the entire night amidst the ghosts of past pupils.

'Mercy goodness me!' he exclaimed in a startled voice, as if he too had seen a ghost. 'Are you still here, lassie? Away home as fast as you can.'

And that was it. No red-hot pokers, no thumb-screws, not even the tawse or a tongue-lashing. It was a tame ending, but at least I had left my mark behind on the floor, and it was good practice with the pen.

3. Growing Pains

Whenever I think of the dentist it is always in French.

Not that ours was a foreigner. He came from Kelso once a week to perform his dark deeds in hired rooms overlooking Jedburgh Abbey. Many a time have I stared in despair at the ruined walls across the way while Mr Crow, foot on pedal, set his whirring drill in motion inside my mouth, Or, worse, extracted a nerve.

'There! It didn't hurt much, did it?'

True, it never hurt him.

Robert Burns knew what he was talking about when he described toothache as 'the hell o' a' diseases'. He even went the length of writing a poem about it. That was what I liked so much about him, he could write about ordinary things. Not just larks soaring in the sky.

> My curse upon your venom'd stang
> That shoots my tortur'd gums alang,

An' thro' my lug gies sic a twang
Wi' gnawing vengeance,
Tearing my nerves wi' bitter pang
Like traction engines.

I wondered if he had ever tried any of Jessie's cures. Sometimes she tied a woollen stocking round my jaw in the hope that the heat would bring relief. A spoonful of whisky held in the decayed tooth was supposed to do the trick, but the taste was terrible when the fiery liquid trickled down my throat, though Robert Burns would doubtless have enjoyed it. In my case it seemed there was no cure for the hell o' a' diseases but to make the dreaded appointment with the dentist.

He was a nice enough wee man, Mr Crow, humming ' 'Way down upon the Swannee River' while he mixed strange concoctions with a small spatula, prior to filling up the holes he had drilled in my teeth. Meanwhile my mouth was gagged with cottonwool which made it difficult to answer his inevitable questions.

'Getting on all right at school?'

'Glug.'

'Going on holiday?'

Shake of the head.

'Is the harvest in yet?'

Half in. How could one answer that? An eye-blink was the best I could do.

'Top of the class yet?'

Top of the class! What a hope! By now he had a half-nelson round my throat and I could neither glug nor blink. All the same, though not anywhere near the heights, I could have told him I was making some progress up the ladder of learning.

Now that I was in the Grammar School, I was a woman of the world, travelling every day to the big town by a bus which I boarded at the roadend a mile away from home.

Old enough to be entrusted with messages to do in the shops during my lunch break. I took tackety boots to be mended at the cobbler's, matched wool, bought kippers, even chose new stays for the cottage wives and long drawers for the herd.

The stir of the traffic no longer held any terrors for me. I had become accustomed to being jostled on the pavement and to hearing Bobby the Bellman shouting out his announcements. 'There will be a stoppage of watterrrr for two hourrrrs. You have been warrrrned.' But I was still a country mouse at heart and my real life was at home on the farm at nights and at the weekends. The rest was only a confused dream. Sometimes more like a nightmare.

I tried hard to get to grips with the perplexing pattern of ever-changing classes at the Grammar School, my mind darting from algebra to science, then on to French, history and Latin. Auld Baldy-Heid had knocked the essentials into me at the village school, but here the methods were very different. And so were the teachers, all with their own quirks. It would take a lifetime, I felt, to sort them out. Especially Mr Archie-Bald, the rector – Dafty, as he was known behind his back – who grew more and more remote, only occasionally coming to life in the Latin class when he lashed out at us with his tongue, threatening to roast us alive or skin the hides off us. A fate not far removed from the tortures of Latin grammar.

Part of my problem was that there was no one at home with whom I could discuss my troubles. Sometimes Mother would ask in an abstracted way: 'How did you get on today?' It was easier just to say 'Fine' than go into details about declensions I could not comprehend, or tell her that the drawing-teacher thought my perspective was up the pole, and that Mary-Ann Crichton had said I did not know an isosceles triangle from a rabbit's foot.

She was our best teacher, Miss Crichton, in spite of her

constant catarrh and her North-East twang which we sometimes found difficult to understand. French and algebra. I was learning a little about the former though my pronunciation – and Miss Crichton's – was further up the pole than my perspective. But set-squares and hypotenuses left me in limbo. I could never see the point of them. What use would they be to me in later life if I was going to follow either of my chosen professions? To be a bondager like Jessie and Joo-anne, or a writer like Anon. They got on fine without square roots.

It was Miss Crichton who first made me think of the dentist in French, and all because of one of her schemes to knock the language into our thick heads. Now that we had progressed a step or two beyond *sur la table* she decided to widen our horizons by making us take part in a simple little French play.

Simple! It was entitled *Madame Lemoine chez le dentiste* and I am never likely to forget it. Even now on sleepless nights I repeat snatches of it to my pillow, hoping it will act as a soporific, but it never does. I grow wider awake as that scene in the classroom comes back to me, so vividly that I can hear Miss Crichton's sniffles, see her hankies drying on the radiator, and cringe as she raps her cane over my knuckles.

'*Non, non! Stupide! Commencez* again.'

We had to take turns at being the hapless Madame Lemoine, which involved going out of the classroom, knocking on the door and waiting for someone to call '*Entrez!*'

Once inside, Madame L. was overcome by fright, easy enough to simulate in my case. The next step was to gaze around the dentist's waiting-room and give voice to a few disjointed observations.

'*Beaucoup de livres sur la table. Des journaux illustrés, mais je n'ai pas envie de lire.*' A few sighs and groans. She wants to escape. What is the time? '*Si seulement je savais*

36

l'heure. Mais il est à remarquer qu'il y a rarement des pendules chez le dentiste . . . '

One dreadful day when the fates were against me there arrived at the Grammar School a real Frenchman. Tight-waisted, pink-cheeked, red-lipped, and with a natty jet-black moustache. The first pretty man I had ever seen. I could visualise him in miniature standing on the mantel-piece made of porcelain. Or perhaps two of him as book-ends.

What was this bright bird of Paradise doing in the Scottish Borders so far away from the Eiffel Tower? The hows and whys we never found out, but it appeared the main purpose of his visit was to assess our progress in his native language. Truth to tell, we thought he had made little progress himself, since his accent was not a patch on Miss Crichton's. He spoke, too, at such a speed, rolling his rs like a Geordie, that it was almost impossible to under-stand a word he said. But Mary-Ann Crichton was not put off. She was determined to put us through our paces and let the Frenchman see we could even *act* in his language.

We all slouched in our seats, hoping not to be called upon, while the Frenchman flashed his eyes and settled down to be entertained. What on earth could have pos-sessed Miss Crichton to single me out to play the part of Madame Lemoine? I would willingly have changed places with a prisoner in the death-cell, but there was no escape.

'*Allez!* Out the door!' she ordered me; and away I trailed, conscious of the Frenchie's amused glance following me.

I stood shivering in the corridor for some time trying to gather up enough courage to knock. Then Miss Crichton called in a commanding voice from inside. '*Frappez!*' I took a deep breath and frapped at the door.

'*Entrez!*'

A scared voice invited me to come in. Jeannie, one of my classmates, had been chosen to be the dentist's assistant, and was trembling with stage-fright, though not half as terrified as I was now that the moment had come when I must make my dreaded entrance. I was about to turn the handle when I was aware of someone looming up behind me. Mr Archie-Bald, the rector.

Dafty had a habit of appearing like ectoplasm when least expected after stalking along passages as silent as a cat.

'You!' he roared, grabbing me by the arm. Dafty never bothered to find out anyone's name. We were all addressed as 'You' or 'Idiot'. He glared at me and demanded, 'What are you doing outside the classroom?'

'Please s-sir, *je suis* Madame Lemoine . . .'

It seemed difficult, even impossible, to tell him either in French or English why I was there. One cannot argue with God.

But now that I was there Dafty suddenly decided he had a use for me. I could hear Jeannie from inside repeating in a frightened voice: '*Entrez! Entrez!*' but there was no escaping Archie-Bald's vice-like grip. 'You'll do,' he said, shaking me loose, 'seeing you're out of the classroom already. Go and find the janitor and tell him to come to my room at once.'

'But, please s-sir, *je suis* . . .'

'At once!' roared Dafty, pointing dramatically down the corridor. 'Go!'

So I went.

There was no knowing where the Janny might be found if he chose to remain invisible. There were so many hidey-holes where he could take cover. In cupboards where he kept cleaning-materials, in store-rooms, or sheds out in the playground. He might even have plunked and gone home for all I knew. It was like playing hide and seek with a slippery eel.

All the while I could sense Miss Crichton's wrath rising to the boil and hear the smiling Frenchie making joking remarks in his strange tongue. How he would roll his

eyes and his rs. As for poor Jeannie, was she still calling
'*Entrez!*' in a despairing voice?

I finally found the Janny in hell, away down in the
nether regions of the boiler house, sitting on a pile of coke
reading an old copy of the Jethart Squeaker. He was not a
bit pleased to see me.

'*Je suis* Madame . . . ' I began. 'I mean, Dafty wants you
in his room. At once.'

The Janny said a bad word and threw his paper aside.
'You're naethin' but a nuisance,' he told me, which I
thought was not quite fair, since I was merely a messenger
from above. 'Get oot ma road.' And away he went, rum-
bling and grumbling, leaving me alone in hell.

I was too shaken to go back to the classroom imme-
diately so I sat down on the coke and had a look at the
Squeaker, turning the pages to see if by chance it was the
one with my name in it, but it wasn't. Fifty years ago, I
learned, there had been a torrential downpour of rain in
Jedburgh, with the High Street awash, shoppers stranded,
and a swan seen swimming in the direction of the Free
Church. Fancy that!

By the time I had summoned up enough courage to go
back, the class had gone off to science. As for the Frenchie,
I never set eyes on him or his wee moustache again. But
retribution, of course, overtook me later when Miss
Crichton, snorting with rage, gave me my character in no
uncertain terms. I did try to explain but it was no use. As
part of my punishment she made me write out Madame
Lemoine's soliloquy a dozen times or more. Little wonder
it is so indelibly fixed in my memory. Yet, though I now
knew the part better than any of my classmates, I was
never again chosen to play Madame L.

Oh well! that, I supposed, was life.

Not real life, though. That was lived in a shabby old
farmhouse in sight of the Cheviots, or out on a windy
hillside in my own ruined castle, surrounded by beasts, as

Jessie called all the creatures on the farm, whether bantams or carthorses. I sometimes envied them their lot. No teachers to chivvy them, no foreign languages to learn, no lines to write. But what a lot they missed, particularly the pleasures of reading.

The great boon of going to the Grammar School was that I could now borrow books from the school library. I had long ago swallowed up every item of literature to be found at home, from *The Wide Wide World* to Spurgeon's *Sermons*. Sometimes I found a tawdry novelette discarded by one of the servant-lasses – *Love Conquers All* – and read it at a gulp. On the whole I preferred *Enquire Within Upon Everything*, even though it concentrated on how to take stains out of tablecloths.

'I've got something in the hoose ye might like,' Jessie said to me one day out of the blue.

'Oh, what is't, Jessie?'

'A book.'

'A book! Could I borrow it, please?'

'Daursay. I'll bring it the morn.'

But the morn seemed a million years away. 'Could I not come and get it tonight?' I pleaded.

Jessie hesitated as if hunting in her mind for the book. Was it maybe in the wall press or below the box bed? I had never seen any reading material in the herd's hoose other than the *People's Friend*, the Squeaker and the bible.

'Please yoursel',' said Jessie, having obviously tracked down the book in its hiding-place. 'But ye're no' to mak' a slaister on't. I'll pit a broon paper cover on its batters.'

'I'll be careful, Jessie. What's it called?''

'Wait an' see. It's a guid read.'

When I rapped on her cottage door that night Jessie did not invite me in. She had the book ready in her hand and passed it out to me with another reminder not get it into a slaister. Behind her I could see into the lamplit kitchen. A quiet scene. Jock sitting by the fire unlacing his boots and Joo-anne bolt upright on a hard chair knitting a long black stocking. A savoury smell lingered about the place. Stovies. The dishes were still on the table, and Jessie had her apron on, ready to tackle the washing-up. So she had no time for small talk with me.

'Awa' hame, lassie.'

It was tantalising not to see even the title of the book in the darkness. The moon was hidden and there was scarcely a star in the sky, so I sped homeward at a spanking pace and hardly drew breath till I tumbled down on the kitchen rug beside Blackie the cat. I opened the book at the title page, drew a deep breath and settled down for a good read.

Seldom if ever have I experienced such a blank feeling of disappointment as I did at that moment when I read the title. Only one word. *Dictionary*. I could scarcely keep back my tears and would have flung the book into the flames had I not feared Jessie's wrath. Was this her idea of a good read? Certainly it contained plenty of words, but what were words to me if not put together in the right way to form a story?

Could this be what Jessie meant? 'Get on wi't, wumman, an' write your ain stories.' Sitting sulkily beside the cat I idly turned a few pages. There was a name written on the fly-leaf. J. Taylor. Jessie? Joo-anne? Jock? A communal schoolbook, perhaps. If so, what care the three had taken of it. No smudges, scribbles, inkblots or torn pages. No despairing calls of 'Help!' as in mine. 'Auld Baldy-Heid's a monster.' 'I'm fed UP.' Every page was pristine. If any had been turned at all, it must have been with the cleanest hands.

Next morning I found it difficult to face Jessie and did not even look at her when she placed my plate of porridge beside me. But when she dumped something else on the table my whole world lit up. It was a book, covered like the dictionary in brown paper, but this was a real storybook with a title. *The Mill on the Floss*, by George Eliot.

'I gied ye the wrang ane last nicht,' said Jessie gruffly. She was not one to apologise. 'Took it oot the room press in the derk, withoot ma specs. Here ye are. It's a guid read.'

A good read!

It was a blessing it was Saturday when I was free to sit on the swing for hours engrossed in the lives of Maggie Tulliver and her brother Tom, described so vividly that I felt I knew them. They might have lived at Edgerston and gone to the village school with me. George Eliot, I felt sure, must be the most wonderful writer in the world, but I thought that of every new discovery.

All that day I was oblivious to the rest of the world; cocks and hens cackling around me, the bubblyjock pecking at my feet, pigs squealing, dogs barking, carthorses clumping in from the fields, till I was pestered by a small lisping child from one of the cottages.

'Will ye come an' play hide-an'-theek?'

'No, I'll not,' I said heartlessly and ran off to my own private refuge on the hill, where I spent the rest of the day crouching amongst the old stones in the great fireplace of the ruined castle. Reading, reading, reading.

'Man-lassie, your een'll drap oot,' said Jock-the-herd who had observed me from a distance and was now leaning on his crook to light his pipe. When I looked up at him *he* seemed someone from another world, not half as real as the characters in the book. But nothing could stop me in my headlong hurry to see what happened next. Later I would start all over again at the beginning to pick up any scraps I had missed. Like second-day soup, there was always a richer flavour in a re-read book. Though nothing, of course, could beat the thrill of first discovery, the finding in the school library of such treasures as *Black Beauty*, *Lorna Doone*, and *David Copperfield*.

It was a meagre enough library. Only a shelf or two in a classroom cupboard, supervised by Miss Paleface, the

English teacher, who made a great fetish of entering our names in a special ledger, noting the dates when we withdrew the books and when they were due to be returned. We were only allowed one a week. I wished it could have been one a day, and was always the first to queue up at the cupboard.

'You'll take care of it, won't you?' said Miss Paleface in her genteel voice. She was much too ladylike to use the word slaister but I knew what she meant and did my utmost to return the books unblemished. It was not easy, reading as I did at the kitchen table or in any hole and corner where I could find sanctuary. All too often the books were splashed with grease, gravy, porridge, or blobs of raspberry jam, and had to go through a great cleaning-up process before they were fit to return.

I can never forget the awful day when *Little Women* fell into the pigs' pail. My own fault. I had left it at the corner of the back-kitchen table where I had been sitting reading amongst the clutter of dirty dishes waiting to be washed, when the telephone rang. It gave me a great sense of importance if I was the only one at home to answer the call. True, Liz-Ann, the Carthorse, was clattering about in the kitchen but she was less likely to lift the receiver than Blackie the cat. So it was left to me.

When I heard Bella's voice from the Post Office I knew I was in for a long session. Goodbye Jo, Beth and all the rest. Real-life drama was happening in Camptown, the small village about a mile away; and though Bella was disappointed that it was only me and not Mother at the end of the line, she gave me chapter and verse, leaving no word unsaid.

'Ye'll never guess! Ye ken Mary-Ann at the lodge gates? Her an' her hens. A'weel, ane o' them's been run ower. By a coal lorry. She's awfu' upset.'

'The hen?'

'No, no; Mary-Ann. The hen's deid. It was ane o' her

43

favourites. Teenie. The wee speckled ane. Puir sowl! she's in a terrible state . . . '

It was ages before the saga of Teenie came to an end, by which time the dirty dishes had been washed and Liz-Ann had gone out to feed the pig. No sign of *Little Women* on the back-kitchen table.

After a distracted search I faced the Carthorse accusingly when she came trailing in.

'Where's my book?'

'Dinna ken. Never seen it.'

'You have sot!'

'Have not!'

Then the terrible truth hit me. It had tumbled into the pigs' pail and was now lost amongst the swill.

I tore round to the sty to discover Grumphy routing about in the trough in company with half a dozen squealing piglets. The sow was greedily gulping down the unsavoury mixture of left-overs that boosted her daily diet. Potato peelings, cabbage leaves, porridge, bread crusts, stale cake. And *Little Women*! Now and again Grumphy sniffed enquiringly at the book and gave an angry grunt when I snatched it up from under her nose.

It was beyond being in a slaister. I washed it, dried it in the oven, rubbed it down with scented soap and recovered it with brown paper, but it still looked a sorry sight when I returned it in fear and trembling to Miss Paleface.

It was the pained expression on her face that hurt me most. Far worse than the ticking off I deserved.

'It was an – an Accident,' I told her. I really could not go into all the unpleasant details about the pigs' pail, and wished she would just punish me and be done with it. But instead she sighed and looked at me so reproachfully that it cut me to the quick. And then, to my horror, Archie-Bald made one of his sudden appearances.

'What,' he demanded, 'has happened to that book?

How did it get into such a dreadful mess? Tell me that.'

There was no escape. I was about to launch into a truthful explanation when to my complete amazement, Miss Paleface spoke up.

'I'm afraid it was my fault, Mr Archibald. I took it home to put a new cover on it and must have left it lying about. My puppy-dog got hold of it and began to chew it up. See what a mess he made! It was very careless of me.'

'Very careless,' agreed Dafty, glaring at her. 'Oh well, you'd better get a replacement.' With that he turned on his heel and went away.

I was too thunderstruck to say anything. I felt my face flushing with embarrassment and could not meet Miss Paleface's gaze. Fancy telling all those black lies! Even though she had done it to save my skin, somehow I never felt the same for her again.

It was the first time I had heard a grown-up tell a deliberate untruth. But it was not to be the last. I was still under the domination of my elders. But were they so infallible? I was beginning to see chinks in their armour. Even Jessie's.

4. Playing the Game

The first time I saw Father set off to go to a rugby match it surprised me that he did not take a gun under his arm. Not even a fishing-rod in his hand, a snare or a ferret in his pocket.

I was only a toddler at the time and had no idea what rugby was, except that it had something to do with sport and that was synonymous with killing. So I expected Father to come home with a brace of something feathered or furry.

'Did you not get any?' I remember asking him when he returned empty-handed.

Father shook his head sadly. 'We lost,' he sighed, and was down in the dumps for the rest of the day.

As I grew older I soon came to grips with the great Border game. It was not long before I became familiar with the fluctuating fortunes of Jedforest, Hawick, Selkirk, Kelso, Gala, Melrose, Langholm and all the rest. Rugger was the same thing but it was mostly university or college

46

chaps who called it that. Rugby was good enough for us.

But it was a man's game, discussed in great detail where two or three were gathered together. The finer points of rucks and scrums were thought to be above the grasp of the female intellect, though some women were allowed to accompany their men to a match, for the sake of an outing, but not to make any comment or ask foolish questions.

'Oh Archie! what's that man doing?'

'Hold your tongue, woman!'

Usually they had the sense to sit mim-mouthed with only an occasional gasp when a player fell flat on his face or had his jersey torn off. Sometimes his breeks, too, at which point the others would discreetly gather round him till someone came running on to the field waving a new pair.

There was great wear and tear, not only of garments, but of arms, legs and collar-bones. It was a poor match if there were not at least one bloodied nose and a broken ankle. Few of the players who ran on to the field at the start could do more than limp off at the end, if not carried on a stretcher. But the wounds were all honourable, and every detail was reported at great length in the Jethart Squeaker. Famous Victory for Jedforest. Or, more often, A Sad Defeat.

I began to read about it myself, striving to figure out the difference between a forward and a scrum-half, why a score was called a try and why the spectators sat on something called a stand. Time and again I pestered Father to take me to a match so that I could solve some of the mysteries. His answer was always the same. 'It's not a game for lasses,' which, of course, only made it sound more desirable.

Occasionally my mother accompanied him 'just for the jaunt', but more often stopped off in the High Street to look at the shops or to visit friends; for, she confessed, if she went to the match she spent most of her time sitting with her eyes shut to avoid seeing the slaughter.

It was a great day for me when Father finally gave in and said, 'Oh well, you can come if you like, if you promise to keep quiet.'

It was mid-winter, bitterly cold, with a flurry of snow in the air, a day for the chimney-corner rather than a chilly rugby field, but nothing would dampen my enthusiasm. Certainly not Jessie's warnings that I would catch my death of cold. Excitement was as good as central-heating, but to please her I took my muff with me to keep my gloved hands warm, and a woolly gravat to wind round my neck.

'Ye'd be the better o' a het-waitter bottle,' she said as I mounted into the gig. 'I'm warnin' ye, lassie, ye'll get nae sympathy if ye come hame deid.'

It was in the days before father's first motor-car, so we drove in the open trap drawn by Flora the white pony. Always at her friskiest in nippy weather, she high-stepped her way in the Jed road like a racehorse, stopping only once for a drink at a trough. It was always Flora who set her own pace and who decided when to swerve in at the roadside to slake her thirst at one of the horse-troughs. She knew them all, and would choose her pick as the fancy took her.

I felt proud to be sitting in front like a lady beside my father instead of in my usual humbler place at the back, often in danger of being flung out if the pony pranced round a corner too quickly. There was not much conversation. I had promised to keep quiet, so I did. I was accustomed, in any case, to keeping my own counsel, and was content enough to sit still watching Flora's steady progress between the shafts. Father held the reins lightly in his hands. He had a whip stuck at the side of the gig but he never used it. 'Steady, lass,' he would say now and again, but that was the only guidance Flora needed. Sometimes he whistled through his teeth or sang a snatch of one of his comic songs.

> Farewell! Farewell! Farewell my fairy fay.
> Oh I'm off to Louisiana
> For to see my Susy Anna,
> Singing Polly wolly doodle all the day.

When we reached Jedburgh Father drew in to the side of the High Street and went off on a mysterious mission, leaving me with the reins to hold. A petrifying moment. What if Flora took it into her head to bolt? I saw myself tugging desperately at the reins while she galloped down the street scattering pedestrians out of her path, knocking cyclists flying and careering over the Old Brig where I would tumble out and land headfirst in the Witches' Pool. Or maybe she would turn round and canter home to the farm, leaving father stranded and me bereft of my rugby match.

She did turn round once but only to give a whinny and look at me with a puzzled expression as if asking, 'Where's the Boss?' At which point he came back, to my great relief, mounted into the gig and handed me a bag of sweets.

'There, lass.'

'Oh, thanks!'

They were mixed chocolates, the kind I could never afford to buy for myself, quantity rather than quality governing my choice. Here I was blessed with both, some covered in silver paper, some in gold. As I peered inside the poke, the game of rugby rose even higher in my estimation.

We had to stable the pony and walk the rest of the way to the field, along with other groups aiming in the same direction. By now my excitement was mounting to such a pitch that Jessie need not have worried about the cold. If there was an icy wind blowing I did not notice it.

Father bought the tickets and we went and sat on the stand, which I still thought was a strange name, while others stood around the pitch stamping their feet to keep warm, impatient for the game to begin. I looked around at everything and everybody. Even the goalposts seemed interesting. I recognised some of the neighbouring farmers, and, hardly believing my eyes, the minister muffled to the ears in a topcoat, with a woollen tammy on his head. Not a sign of his dog-collar.

I was so busy looking at him that I almost missed the entry of the gladiators who were suddenly on the field running about in all directions, some with striped jerseys and some in plain colours. Good men and true, with bandaged heads and knees from previous battles, but all ready to fight it out to the bitter end.

Even the beginning seemed fierce enough. I thought the game had started but they were only knocking up. Suddenly the referee, an overgrown schoolboy in shorts, called them to order and blew a blast on his whistle. The crowd cheered, the minister jiggled up and down in his seat, and from then on so many things happened that I found it difficult to keep track of events. So did the reporter from the Squeaker who ran hither and thither round the sidelines like a mad grasshopper in his efforts not to miss a paragraph. It was a dangerous assignment for him, especially when a zealous player, chasing the ball, collided with him outside the touchline, sending him flying in one direction and his notebook in another. I wondered if he would include the episode in next week's report – Jedforest Scrapes Through – but for some reason he left it out.

Not that there was any dearth of incidents. I could see why Mother kept her eyes shut. I had to clap my muff to my mouth to prevent myself from gasping, 'Oh mercy me!' every time a couple of players barged into each other and I could hear their heads cracking. Sometimes one would lie dead on the field till a wee man came running on and squeezed a wet sponge down the back of his neck, whereupon the corpse suddenly sprang to life, shook himself like a terrier, and dived into the scrum as large as life.

At times the referee blew angry blasts on his whistle, pointed a furious finger at the players and appeared to be giving them a sound telling-off. But he, too, was frequently felled to the ground when he got in their way, and was limping like the rest before the game was through.

In the first half the striped lot were winning. Father was groaning and the minister behaving in a very un-ecclesiastical manner, shouting advice to the Jedforest team and abuse at the referee. Sometimes he clutched his tammy in despair and hid his face in his hands. I contemplated passing him a chocolate, but I doubt if even a raspberry cream would have consoled him.

At half-time the teams had a brief respite when they stood in separate huddles, and sucked lemons, the very sight of which drew my mouth together, though there was a caramel in it at the time. Then they changed ends and continued the fray with such vigour that one of the players was carried off on a stretcher and the referee had to run about holding a hankie to his nose to stem the bleeding. Meantime, the snow, which had been drifting down in dribbles, began to fall in earnest, though no one seemed to take any notice of it. It would have taken an earthquake at least to have stopped the match, especially near the end when Jedforest's fortunes were on the turn.

When the game was clinched by a drop-goal the Jed supporters exploded. Father cheered. The minister tossed his tammy in the air and shook hands with himself. I swallowed my sweetie, and the victorious players, ignoring their wounds, ran off the field looking modestly pleased with themselves. It was all over, except for traces of blood splashed on the snow.

We gave the minister a lift home and I was relegated to the back of the gig with his bicycle tied on with binder-twine. It kept me from tumbling out when Flora took to her heels and went speeding away home through the snowy darkness. The air was thick with flakes which froze on my cheeks as they fell, but I still had my inner warmth and the sound of 'Come on, Jed!' ringing in my ears. I felt that I had been blooded and was now an expert in the magic game of rugby.

This, of course, was big-time stuff. My own games consisted of more solitary pursuits. Skipping, swinging, playing with a tennis ball, if I could find one not already burst. When all else failed Jessie sometimes made one for me out of old newspapers, rolling pages of the *Scotsman* and the Squeaker together, moulding them into a more or less rounded object.

'It'll kep a catch,' she would say, meaning it would do for the time being, and so it did. I had many hours of pleasure tossing it up into the air and retrieving it as it came down. But a real 'stotting' ball was best, one that could be bounced against the stone walls of the house, or thrown up on the roof to come trickling down, if it did not stick in the rone-pipe. Then I would have to coax the herd to bring out the long ladder from the cartshed and climb up to rescue it.

'Man-lassie! ye're mair bother than a cairtload o' monkeys,' he would grumble, but he never refused.

There were endless permutations in throwing and catching, and a certain ritual known to all Border bairns who chanted the words as they went through the different sequences.

> Plainy.
> Clappy.
> Roll the pirrn.
> Backy.
> Little ball.
> Big ball.
> Clitchie-clatch.
> Briestie.
> Birly.

The last was the most difficult as one had to twirl round while the ball was in midair and be ready to catch it as it fell down. I wondered if the rugby team went through a similar exercise when they were training, or if they just practised kicking each other on the shins.

Kick-the-can, bar-the-door, tig, and cuddy-loup-the-dyke (leapfrog) were great favourites in the school playground, but these were communal games. There was little fun playing hide-and-seek by myself, though the farmyard was a great place for such a pursuit, full of hidey-holes where one could lie undetected for hours: in the caff-hole amongst the chaff, inside an empty water-barrel, under a reaper in the cartshed, behind the harness in the work-stable, up a tree, or burrowed beneath the straw in the barn.

Sometimes I prevailed on Wee Maggie from the cottages to play but she could never find me, and grew tearful as she wandered desolately around the place. 'Where aboot are ye? Am I gettin' warm?' In the end I always gave myself up, out of pity for her. She, on the other hand, had no notion how to conceal herself and always gave the show away by giggling, or calling out: 'I'm here! Ahint the henhoose.'

My favourite solitary ploy was running with a gird, a gird simply being an old wheel or hoop which could be guided by a stick, or better still an iron cleek. There was a great art in guiding the gird to make it run smoothly and steadily without veering off to one side or another, though in my case, because of the bumpiness of the farm road, it more often ended in the ditch. But on the occasions when I ventured as far as the roadend and out on to the main road, the gird went spinning away in front of me at such a rate that I had great difficulty in keeping up with it.

Somehow, because it was so absorbing, I never noticed how many miles I ran. It was almost as good as getting a hurl.

'Are you going to walk there?' I once heard someone asking Big Bob when he had been sent on a message.

'Walk? Nae fears! I'm gaun to rin wi' ma gird.'

Big Bob's gird was his pride and joy, a perfectly rounded wheel with a splendid cleek to go with it, unlike my own dented object which became so battered and bent that it could only zig-zag across the road. In the end it called for great ingenuity to make it move at all, and I begged Jock-the-herd to find me a replacement.

'Man-lassie, whaur'll I get a wheel? Aff a cairt?'

But a cartwheel was too big and too heavy. For a time I had to be content with a small pram-wheel which went dancing and prancing away in front of me at such a speed that it was impossible to keep up with it. Then one day Jock discovered a discarded wheel from an old bicycle which had belonged to one of the hinds.

'The verra dab!' said he, straightening the spokes. 'There! that'll dae ye.'

It did me all right. Though I could never compete with Big Bob – I had only a wooden stick instead of a proper cleek – I became so attached to my gird that it was almost like guiding a live thing which jumped and jouked in front of me, with a decided personality of its own. I could have run, I felt sure, all the way to Jedburgh with it and never noticed the distance.

Parlour games could be hitty-missy if grown-ups were involved, playing down to the smaller fry and doing their best to lose. I hated when they cheated at tiddlywinks or ludo. 'Good for you! You've won again.' This was no use. I preferred a straight contest, whether I won or not, and always as a child longed to be treated rationally whether in conversation or playing a game of snakes and ladders.

On one never-to-be-forgotten occasion all the children in the district were bidden by the laird to attend a Christmas party at the Big Hoose at Edgerston. This was equivalent to being invited by God to enter heaven and play with the angels. Few of us had set foot in the mansion house before and had no idea what to expect as we wended our ways down the drive, uncomfortably attired in our best clothes and with parental warnings ringing in our ears. Dire threats of what would happen to us if we made a noise, a mess, spoke unless spoken to, ate too much, or behaved in any way normally. Had we obeyed them to the letter we would all have sat like stookies neither moving nor uttering a word.

Jessie had tried to feed me with porridge before I left home to take the edge off my appetite. 'It'll fill up your waim.' But I was far too excited to swallow a spoonful.

My hair had been brushed and combed to take all the tangles out – the 'rugs', Jessie called them – before being tightly plaited and tied with new blue ribbons at the ends. I would get murdered, I was told, if I lost them or scuffed my new shoes. Shiny black patent leather, fit for Buckingham Palace let alone the Big Hoose. Little did I know until I changed into them that they were as slippery as eels and that the polished floor was like a skating-rink. Every time I moved my feet slid from me in different directions. In the first few minutes I took several tumbles under the amused gaze of the gentry, and blushed scarlet with shame, hoping my parents would never hear of my downfall.

When I was in an upright position my attention was riveted on the glittering chandeliers that hung from the ceiling in the centre of the big room where we were assembled. Real electric light, not paraffin lamps or candles; also on the Christmas tree that stood in the corner bedecked with tinsel and coloured lights. There was a fairy doll perched on the topmost branch stretching out her gauzy wings as if poised for flight. None of us had ever seen anything like it before. We could only gaze in admiration, wondering how an ordinary fir tree grown in the Edgerston woods could possibly have undergone such a transformation.

It was quite easy to guess who Santa Claus was when he came in wearing a red cloak, a false beard and his own aquiline nose. No disguise could conceal the laird's London voice as he handed out presents to us all and said a few words to each of us. Not that we understood them. It was difficult at the best of times to know what he was saying; and now, speaking through his beard, it was impossible. But at least we all got gifts, presented with a fine disregard as to their suitability.

Big Bob, for example, was handed a dolls' teaset and Chrissie Smith, a toddler from Camptown, fell heir to a toy pistol with caps. Amongst the other items given away holus-bolus were mouth-organs, a jack-in-the-box, a teddy bear, skipping-ropes, a sewing-set, and a box of toy soldiers. When my turn came I slid towards Santa in my slippery shoes – indeed, I almost slid past him – and was presented with a catapult which I later swapped with Big Bob for his dolls' teaset. To this day I keep the cracked creamjug on a shelf, a reminder of many an imaginary teaparty held long ago in my castle on the hill, with unseen guests sipping from the cups and eating non-existent sandwiches from the miniature plates.

It was when we started playing games that I knew there was no hope for me unless I discarded my shoes, so I kicked them off and went round the Mulberry Bush in my stocking-soles. It did no good to the stockings and I paid dearly for my sins when I got home, but for the time being I felt free to gallop with the rest in the Grand Old Duke of York and Through the Needle's Eye, Boys.

At intervals the laird's house-guests, who were organising the festivities, would ask one or other of us, 'What would you like to do next, dear?' To which, when it came to his turn, Big Bob replied truthfully, 'Gang hame.'

I was sorry Sir J. M. Barrie was not staying at the Big Hoose, as he sometimes did. I had a feeling he would have had some daft tricks up his sleeve to enliven the proceedings which tailed off after a tepid game of Blind Man's Buff, during which we were afraid to move lest we crashed into any of the priceless objects displayed around the various polished tables. It was difficult to let oneself go in such surroundings. Even the fancy spread, with shivery jellies, trifles and wee iced cakes, was not to the liking of one shepherd's bairn, who, having stuffed himself with what he considered rubbish, demanded 'a slice o' plain breid'. And though it had been a great occasion, one to be talked about for weeks afterwards, we all felt a sense of relief when it was over and we were free to go home.

Organised games, I decided, were not for me. I was so used to my own solitary pursuits. Winter was a great time for sledging, sliding and snowballing. Even the hinds and the herd would scoop up handfuls of snow to fling at each other, or slither in their tackety boots down a long slippery slide, arms outstretched to balance themselves. It was great to hear them whooping like children and to know that, old though they were, they still had a spark inside them.

5. Ewe-lamb

My dream in those far off days was to be an only child,
not just one of a litter. It would be wonderful, I thought,
to be the sole object of my parents' care, all attention
riveted on me, the most important person in the household.
No more hand-me-doons to wear; every whim granted.

It was rare to find such a bairn in the Borders. The
cradle seemed no sooner relegated to the garret than it
was brought down again and the current baby 'shortened',
so that his long clothes – the cumbersome garments into
which every child was tucked and safety-pinned – could be
refurbished to fit the new arrival.

'It's God's will,' Jessie would say, pursing her lips; but
I felt she disapproved of the whole performance. 'Mrs
Scott! She's nae sooner up than she's doon. Aye kittlin',
like the cat.'

My desire to be an only child was sparked off by envy
of a pupil at the Grammar School, the apple of her parents'
eyes. Their one ewe-lamb.

She had a smug look on her face as if she knew she was someone special, as indeed she was. To her doting parents, at least, who could scarcely let her out of their sight. Her mother waited for her at the school gates, sometimes her father, too. Off they would go up the High Street with the ewe-lamb between them, chattering away ten to the dozen and her parents hanging on every word. Imagine being so cherished and having someone to *listen*! I wove many a fantasy about having such love and attention lavished on me.

The ewe-lamb was smaller and neater than I was. 'A dainty wee piece,' Jessie would have called her, with golden ringlets, not a hair out of place, and never a wrinkle in her stockings. I felt an inferior being in her presence, though sometimes she graciously allowed me to pick up her books or help her with her French verbs, not that I was any great shakes at them myself.

She took all homage for granted, as if she had a right to it, and every day she seemed to have a new possession. A hair clasp, a pencil case, a brooch or a bangle, and always a bag of sweets. On special occasions, such as her birthday, she would reel off a list of presents. My own birthday was scarcely noticed at home, far less celebrated with cakes, candles, parties and expensive gifts. But I was not a ewe-lamb.

One day, however, out of the blue there came the chance of a lifetime.

An invitation to spend a week of my holidays in Hawick. No other member of the family was included. They wanted *me* on my own.

Who were they? Aunt Bessie and Uncle Tom, distant relatives, an elderly couple who had once stayed with us at Overton Bush and who now wrote to say they would like to have 'the little lass' on a return visit. I had been like a ray of sunshine, they said, showing them all over the farm, being so bright and helpful that they had taken quite a fancy to me and were now looking forward to showing me the sights of Hawick. If I could be spared!

'Spared!' grumped Jessie before I could get too puffed up with pride. 'Ye'll be a guid riddance. They maun be aff their heids.'

I was nearly off mine with conceit at the thought of being singled out in such a manner. It was the first time I felt I was somebody, and for the next few days I went about with an elevated feeling, superior to everybody.

I had only a hazy recollection of what the elderly couple were like. Uncle Tom, I remembered, had a long white beard like a prophet in the bible and Aunt Bessie was small and rotund, but beyond that my memory was dim, though, of course, they must be specially nice to have noticed my good qualities.

As for Hawick I had no clearer picture of the place. I knew it was the biggest and most stirring town in Roxburghshire, proudly calling itself the Queen of the Borders. The mills were there, mysteriously turning wool into jerseys, jumpers and tweeds. And, of course, there was the monument in the main street with its strange inscription:

Teribus y Terioden
Sons of heroes slain at Flodden.

It was all to do with battles long ago and the gods Thor and Odin whose help the Hawick warriors had invoked when routing a party of English soldiers, returning victorious from Flodden. Revenge was sweet, and every year the incident is commemorated at the Common Riding when the Hawick folk shout out the slogan triumphantly, 'Teerie-bus and Teerie-oden', and are known locally as Teeries or Terriers.

For farming folk Hawick meant the lamb sales. I had once attended them myself, bewildered by the confused dirdum of the livestock market, with frightened lambs bleating piteously, strange collies bowfing at each other, the auctioneer rattling on nonstop, shepherds brandishing their crooks as they drove their flocks round the ring, while farmers waited anxiously to hear the final figure. As the buying and selling proceeded no money seemed to change hands apart from a luck-penny to seal a bargain. But I could tell by the look on Father's face if the price had been favourable. It meant not only much-needed money in his pocket but a feather in his cap – and in Jock-the-herd's – if Overton Bush came out on top. Something to boast about during the year.

On that occasion there had been no opportunity for me to explore the town before we had to set off on the journey home by gig. I sat in the back with Jock who had walked the sheep all the long miles from the farm to Hawick, taking two days on the job, using the drove-roads and staying the night at a friendly farm on the way. According to him, the beasts arrived at the sales in better shape than in later days when they were whisked there in an hour or so in motor-driven lorries, 'shoogled oot their wuts'.

Jock was thankful to get away from the bustle and fell instantly asleep beside me after groaning, 'Sic a steerie! It gaurs ma heid birl. Man-lassie! I'll be gled to get hame to ceevilisation.' I kept a watchful eye on him in case he tumbled out when Flora swerved round a corner. I was used to such misadventures myself, but it would be no easy job hauling the herd back into place. He was a stocky man, as solid as a rock.

Later, when the invitation came and I broke the news to him that I was about to go to Hawick for a week, he stared at me in horror

'A week! In thon noisy toon. Wumman, ye'll no' live to tell the tale.'

'I will so,' I said defiantly. 'It'll be great.'

He shook his head pityingly. 'Puir sowl! I doot if ye'll survive. A hale week!'

He made it sound like a life sentence, but nothing could dim my ardour. I was packed and ready long before the great day when father was to drive me there, this time in the motor. The Tin Lizzie. It was faster than Flora though not so reliable and we had many false starts before we finally saw Ruberslaw looming up in the distance, the rugged hill that dominated the landscape.

> Dark Ruberslaw, that lifts his head sublime,
> Rugged and hoary with the wrecks of time . . .

Why were the hills always male? I wondered. Were there no lasses amongst them?

He – Ruberslaw – had once been a great hiding-place for Covenanters who came there to worship in secret, lurking in furtive little groups on the hillside. I had heard tales of their narrow escapes from their persecutors when mists mysteriously rolled down from heaven to protect them.

It was here, too, in Teviotdale, that the Little Folk lived. Good ones and bad. Some who made crops flourish, others who caused cows to go eild (that is, cease to yield milk), or stole babies away and left wizened changelings in their place. The cure for anyone elf-struck was to gather foxgloves, known as witches' thimbles, and make a magic potion which would cure all ills.

We saw no signs of the Little People as Tin Lizzie rattled her way into Hawick. I was to be deposited at the monument and handed over like a parcel, along with a basket containing fresh butter, eggs and home-made jam, to the elderly couple who would be waiting for me. And there they were, standing patiently beside the mounted warrior, scanning the street for signs of the Tin Lizzie, smiling and waving when it drew up beside them with a screech of brakes.

At first they seemed strangers to me, older even than I had expected, but obviously so pleased to see me that my heart warmed towards them. They thanked Father not only for the basketful of farm fare, but for letting me come. It must be such a sacrifice to him, being left without me for one whole week.

Father looked a trifle surprised at this, and at the last moment thrust his hand into his pocket, jingled around amongst the coins and brought out a fistful of silver which he passed on to me as spending-money. It amounted to almost ten shillings, more than I had ever possessed in my life before. Enough to buy up the whole of Hawick.

I could only gulp my thanks and say 'Ta-ta' when he reversed round the monument and disappeared into the distance with sparks flying from the motor. I had a sudden feeling of alarm, for I was alone now, a stranger in a strange town. Apart, of course, from Aunt Bessie and Uncle Tom, who soon dispelled my fears by taking me by the hand and leading me away up a wynd, round a corner and into their small snug house in a back street.

It was like a house in a fairy-tale, fit for the Little People themselves. Only a but and ben, cluttered with furnishings, footstools, antimacassars, pot plants and ornaments, so crowded that it was dangerous to make a sudden movement for fear of knocking over a vase or bumping into a rocking-chair. Every single space on the walls was covered with pictures and texts. Bless This House. God Is Watching. Be Sure Your Sins Will Find You Out.

There was a fierce fire burning in the grate sending out such a heat that I tried to retreat from it as far as possible, but the tea-table was in the way, spread with all the ingredients for a high tea. Meat pies, sandwiches, currant bread, rock cakes, parkins and cream cookies. We sometimes had plain cookies at home when the vanman called, or even curranty cookies with sugar on top, but these had been split open and were oozing with cream.

'A Hawick speciality,' said Uncle Tom, passing the plate to me. 'Eat up, lass.' He turned to Aunt Bessie. 'She's far too thin, isn't she, Bessie?'

'Ay, the bairn needs fattening.'

They started to talk about me as if I was not there, discussing what they would do to amuse me during the week. Uncle Tom would take me to the park, Aunt Bessie to the shops, and maybe we could visit Cousin Somebody who had a talking budgie. The main thing was that the lass must enjoy herself.

It was great being the sole object of their attention, though what with the extra food I had eaten to please them, and the heat of the fire, I began to feel drowsy. When I closed my eyes for the long grace at the end of the meal, I could happily have floated off into dreamland. But Aunt Bessie began to bustle about, clearing the table, and Uncle Tom put another lump of coal on the fire and said, 'Sit in, lass, an' get warm. Tell us all about everything.'

It was a heady feeling being the centre of attraction. For a time I opened out like a flower, elaborating on every little happening on the farm. My audience was interested in the smallest detail, prompting me to 'Go on, dearie; what happened next?' Uncle Tom kept saying, 'My word, Bessie, she's great company, is she not?'

But I could not keep it up. My head was beginning to nod, and my cheeks were burning from the heat of the fire.

'The bairn's sleepy. She's needing her bed. Light the gas, Tom,' said Aunt Bessie, reaching up to rummage for the matches amongst the ornaments on the mantlepiece. A porcelain pig, a china duck, a cracked vase containing honesty, spectacle cases, keys, and yet another text, The Meek Shall Inherit the Earth.

I forced myself to watch Uncle Tom lighting the gas for I had never witnessed the process before nor heard the hiss-ss-ss when the mantle began to glow. The gas gave out a white light, brighter than our paraffin lamps at home but less kindly. I could see the crumbs on the floor, the rust on the fire-tongs and the fluff that had collected on the mantelpiece. Aunt Bessie was not the best of house-wives.

'I'll just give it a lick and a promise,' she would say each day, flicking the duster here and there; but she was nice for all that, and meek enough to inherit the earth.

I wondered where I was to sleep but the mystery was solved when Uncle Tom suddenly let down a bed from the wall. There it was, all ready for me, complete with patch-work quilt.

'Say your prayers and tuck yourself in. We'll away ben to our own room. Sleep tight, lass, and we'll see you in the morning.'

I kept coming and going all night wondering where I was, in this world or the next. The fire, though shielded by a guard, was still burning brightly, flickering in my eyes. And the grandfather clock in the corner was the busiest I had ever heard, tick-tocking the noisy minutes away and chiming every quarter. I could hear trains in the distance shunting at the station and screaming along the lines. Then Aunt Bessie and Uncle Tom snoring in unison from the adjacent room.

It was an uneasy night. I felt stifled in the claustro-phobic atmosphere and flung aside the patchwork quilt, longing for a gulp of fresh air. I felt apprehensive, too, about the bed, comfortable though it was. What if it sprang up as suddenly as it had been let down, and trapped me against the wall?

When I woke in the morning Aunt Bessie was boiling one of our farm eggs for my breakfast and Uncle Tom had gone off to work. I never knew what he did; something in one of the woollen mills which kept him occupied till he came home for his high tea each evening. So Aunt Bessie and I were left during the day to our own resources.

The housework was soon over. A lick and a promise, then we were free to go out and about. This was what I was longing for. Fresh air; but it was too fresh for Aunt Bessie. We were no sooner outside the door than she began to shiver and dragged me back in again. After rummaging in a drawer she produced a woolly scarf.

'Put that round your throat, dearie, to keep the chill out.'

I was not feeling the chill, but I did as I was bid while she fixed a fur tippet round her throat, and thus fortified we finally sallied forth. I wanted to rush on ahead and see everything all at once, but Aunt Bessie held my hand and I was forced to match my steps to hers.

When we reached the main street we went in and out of several shops. At the baker's I saw cream cookies in the window and was pleased when Aunt Bessie bought some for our tea. In the greengrocer's it took her a long time to decide whether to buy carrots or onions. It seemed strange having to pay for vegetables which grew so plentifully on the farm at home, and all free.

Aunt Bessie had a purse that snapped shut, with separate compartments where the copper coins were segregated from the silver. My own money was burning holes in my pocket. I was eager to spend it but not on carrots and onions. I wanted to be free to run up and down the street, peering at any shop window that took my fancy, but I had to accompany Aunt Bessie to the fishmonger's, hopping from one foot to the other while she swithered between kippers and haddocks.

'Which would you like, dearie? Take your pick. A kipper or a haddock? Or maybe a herring?'

I was not accustomed to being consulted on such matters, or indeed on any others, and at first I enjoyed the sensation of choosing between chops and sausages at the butcher's, or brown bread and white at the baker's; but as time went by I grew impatient with the whole performance and said, 'Oh, I don't mind, Aunt Bessie. Anything you like.'

It was a strange week, the longest I had ever spent in

my life. I kept recalling Jock-the-herd's words. 'A hale week! Ye'll no' live to tell the tale.' Even at the end of the first day I felt I had been away from home for a lifetime. It was wonderful, of course, basking in the old folks' approval. Nothing I said or did was wrong. Not a word of criticism.

I was in great danger of having my head turned, and found myself acting a part so that I could receive even more adulation, colouring everything I said to make it sound more interesting. In other words, showing off. Jessie would have been scunnered with me.

The days began to emerge into a pattern. Mornings spent shopping with Aunt Bessie. Afternoons visiting some of her neighbours and old friends. Old! Everyone I met was ancient, with sunken eyes, wrinkled cheeks, and brown blotches on their shaky hands. The only bright spot was when we visited Cousin Somebody who had a talking budgie. 'I'm a prrr-rrretty wee boy. A prrr-rrretty wee boy.' But I felt sure he would sooner have been a free bird.

Aunt Bessie encouraged me to show off my talents in front of them. 'She can speak *French*,' she would tell them proudly. 'Say something, dearie.'

I felt like the budgie, and said something even if it was only '*Ouvrez la porte*' or a quotation from *Madame Lemoine chez le dentiste*. They all agreed I was a great wee character, and I began to believe it.

Most evenings Uncle Tom took me for a sedate walk to the park. There were swings there, and sometimes he would give me a gentle push to and fro. Not too high in case it made me sick. I did not tell him I had a swing at home which the herd had made for me and that I could fly higher than the treetops without turning a hair. I was getting used to acting a part, becoming a make-believe person unlike my real self.

Sometimes at night when the gas was lit in the overcrowded room Uncle Tom took down an old fiddle from the top of the press and played some scratchy Scottish airs while Aunt Bessie nid-nodded her head in time to the music. Or he would recite one of the long Border ballads which so often ended in tragedy.

> She sought him east, she sought him west,
> She sought him brade and narrow,
> Sine in the clifting of a crag
> She found him drowned in Yarrow.

'Stop it, Tom. Ye'll make the lassie greet,' Aunt Bessie would protest, drying her own eyes. 'Give us another wee tune on the fiddle.'

I did my best to be an interested audience and to take my turn when they asked me to entertain them. They never tired of hearing tales about the farm, about Bella Confectionery at the post office, Auld Baldy-Heid at the village school, or Yorkie the tramp. As for saying my poetry, I recited everything from 'Rainy, Rainy Rattle-stanes' to 'The Lord's My Shepherd', and even tried to sing one of Father's comic songs: 'I'm the saftest o' the faimly'.

I liked best when Uncle Tom told tales of his own childhood when he had brose for breakfast and ran bare-foot to school where he learned to write on a slate. Or about how he had once seen the Kelpie that lived in a nearby loch. He always ended his reminiscences with a jingle.

> That was langsyne when geese were swine
> And turkeys chewed tobacco,
> And sparrows bigget in auld men's beards
> And mowdies delved potatoes.

6. The Ragamuffin

Long before the middle of the week the novelty of being an only child, a ewe-lamb, had worn off, and I began to count not only the days but the hours till Father would come and fetch me home. We were to meet him at the monument where I was to be handed back. What if he did not turn up? The thought became a nightmare to me, and I sent off a postcard, the first I had ever written to him. With a picture of the Teribus Monument on it as an added reminder.

'Dear Father, I will see you on Saturday at three o'clock. Don't forget.' Then, of course, I lied a bit. 'I am having a great time in Hawick.' I was not sure what to put at the end. Yours truly or yours sincerely. So I just repeated 'Don't forget' and left it at that.

'What about staying on for another week?' Uncle Tom suggested.

'Oh yes!' said Aunt Bessie, beaming.

'Oh no!' I said quickly. Too quickly. Then, not to

hurt their feelings, 'It would be lovely but I'm needed at home.' Lying again!

They understood that. How could the family possibly do without me for another seven days? Uncle Tom and Aunt Bessie would just have to make the most of me, they said, for one short week.

Short! Surely no timepiece had ever ticked as slowly, as well as loudly, as the grandfather clock in that stuffy little sitting-room. I felt smothered by the heat, the suffocation of the wall-bed and the over-cossetting of the old people. Killed by kindness.

I ached for the freedom to run outside, or to sit quietly on my own reading a book. There were only three on a dusty shelf: *The Pilgrim's Progress*, the bible, and *Hymns Ancient and Modern*, but I was so starved for words that they were better than nothing. Yet it was impossible for me to cut myself off for long enough to dip into them before Aunt Bessie or Uncle Tom, fearing I must be bored, tried to liven me up by suggesting a game of draughts or dominoes. Uncle Tom always let me win. 'There! she's beaten me again. Isn't she a smart wee lass, Bessie?'

I was becoming listless and finding it more and more difficult to live up to my reputation of being a ray of sunshine when one day Aunt Bessie said, 'I think I'll take a wee nap this afternoon. Will you be all right, dearie?'

'Oh *yes*, Aunt Bessie. Can I go out, please?'

'Well – don't get lost, mind. Put on the woolly scarf . . .'

I was off like an arrow from the bow, running as if I was in a race. Away down the wynd and into the main street. Never mind the fishmonger, the greengrocer, the cream-cookie shop. I made straight for one with Confectionery above the door. Not 'Confectionary', like Bella's at the post office at home.

At last I had the chance to spend some of my wealth. There were sweets I had never seen in the window before.

Hawick balls were the local equivalent of Jethart snails, though quite different, of course. Sugar mice, bon-bons, pink and white coconut ice, nougat, macaroon bars, and dozens of others. A feast for the eyes and a problem when it came to choosing.

After much swithering I went in and bought a bag of mixed caramels, a sugar mouse, a toffee apple, and some extra-strong peppermints for the old folk, the flat pale-brown kind that were good for the wind and brought tears to the eyes. Then, making the most of my freedom, and with a treacle caramel in my mouth, I made my way to the park.

It was here I met the Ragamuffin. He was, I suppose, my first lad, though maybe it was only cupboard-love on his part, for he soon demolished the sugar mouse, the toffee apple and the rest of the caramels, and would have polished off the peppermints as well, if I had not hidden them in my coat pocket.

He had a lean and hungry look about him, like a stray dog searching for scraps. The truth was, he must have been half-starved, poor thing. A skinnymalink of a laddie with holes in his stockings, no elbows in his grubby jersey, and frayed sandshoes tied together with string. But he had a nice mop of curly black hair and an engaging grin. I liked the look of him, and he took to me, too, I think. I hoped it was not only because of my wealth.

We had eyed each other before when I was out with Uncle Tom, but *he* did not think much of the boy.

'He's just scum. Keep away from that ragamuffin,' he warned me. 'He smells.'

True enough he did, but I was used to smells on the farm. I wondered why Uncle Tom who was so fond of quoting texts from the bible – charity suffereth long and is kind – could not find a place in his heart for a ragged laddie. It was a queer thing, religion. If the boy came too near me and tried to get on to the next swing Uncle Tom put on a fierce face and shouted, 'Away you go! Keep your distance from decent folk.'

Today the Ragamuffin and I sat side by side on the swings, sucking our caramels, not saying much but content in each other's company. When he did speak he sometimes said strange things. 'I'm listening to the trees,' cocking his head to one side as if hearing voices. I understood that, for I often listened to the trees myself. Or he would tell lies. Not small tarradiddles but great thumpers, not boasting as Big Bob did, but seeing visions, I suppose.

'Ay, so I wull,' he would say, half to himself, half to me. 'Sail roond the world. An' I'll invent something.'

'What?'

'Canna say till I've invented it.' Then, 'Ma faither's got thoosands o' pounds in the bank. He's a millionaire.'

'Oh yes?' I was not sure if he even had a father.

'Ma mother's a Ladyship.'

'Likely!'

'We've got a muckle big car at hame. *Twa* muckle big cars. Hae ye ony mair sweeties in your pooch?'

When I heard the town clock striking and made a sudden move to hurry home to Aunt Bessie's stuffy little house – back to prison – he looked at me and asked, 'Are ye comin' back the morn?'

'I will if I can,' I promised, and gave him an extra-strong peppermint as a parting gift, then handed him the whole bag. I could always buy some tomorrow for the old folk.

As it happened I was back again that very evening, but not alone. Uncle Tom held me by the hand and the Ragamuffin had enough sense to keep his distance while I pretended not to notice him. It was strange living a double life. Every day when I could escape I ran first to the shops and then to the park. He was always waiting for me to receive any largesse I had in my pockets. We got on a treat, bouncing up and down on the see-saw or swaying on the swings. I never knew his name and he did not ask mine.

As a result of all the mollycoddling meted out to me during that everlasting week I took a cold in my head. Nothing I would even have noticed at home, but the old people were as alarmed as if I had caught galloping consumption and would soon be in my grave. They kept taking my temperature and dosing me with cough-mixture.

'D'you think we should send for the doctor, Tom?' asked Aunt Bessie, looking worried.

The very idea horrified me. 'What? Just for a *cold*!' I said, trying to stifle a sneeze. At home it would have to be a broken collar-bone at least before anyone took such a drastic step. 'It's nothing. I'm ever so much better.' Indeed, the cold would have taken its normal course, I felt sure, if they had ignored it instead of swathing me in shawls, sprinkling my hankies with eucalyptus and drugging me with ipecacuanha wine till I smelt as strongly as the Ragamuffin.

'I'm fine!' I kept protesting. 'Fine!'

One night, with a muffler wrapped round my head and another round my throat, they took me as a treat to a place called the Mission. I had no idea what it would be like. The pictures, maybe, or a sing-song, but it turned out to be a prayer-meeting in a hall where folk got up now and again to 'give their testimony' and tell how they came to be saved. I was terrified the preaching man would call upon me, for I had no idea whether I was saved or not. Likely not, I thought, with all the lies I had been telling lately. Be sure your sins will find you out.

Came the final day at long last. How eagerly I had waited for it. My only regret was that I would have to say goodbye to the Ragamuffin.

I managed to escape on my own to do my final shopping. A bag of cream-cookies to take home to mother – likely they would be squashed to bits by the time I reached the farm – a stucco statue of the monument for Jessie (A Present from Hawick) and a red and white spotted handkerchief for Jock. For Aunt Bessie and Uncle Tom I found a small golden angel in a shop, to put on their dusty mantelpiece. No doubt it would remind them of me. Perfect in every detail, except that I had no wings.

It was difficult to decide what to buy for the Ragamuffin especially as my money was running out. In the end I bought a bar of highly scented soap to sweeten him up and a large bag of liquorice allsorts. I had only sixpence left which I decided to give him as a parting gift.

He was waiting for me in the park, the faithful swain, hanging upside-down from one of the swings like a curly-headed monkey. All the blood had run to his head and his face was bright pink. When he turned himself right way up to receive his gifts, he sniffed at the soap and stuffed it in his pocket before devouring the liquorice allsorts one by one as if he was eating a meal. Maybe he was, poor soul.

The Ragamuffin had a present for me, too; a chuckie-stone veined in various colours. Delicate shades of pink and green and grey. He must have picked it up from a burn and spent hours polishing it till it shone like a precious stone.

'It cost a fortune,' he said, thrusting it into my hand. With a millionaire father and a Ladyship mother, he could well afford it. As for me, I valued the gift for its own sake and for the thought that lay behind it.

I could not face farewells so after a while I just gave him the sixpence, said 'Ta-ta' and went away without looking back. I never saw him again but I treasured the pebble for many a year and often wondered what became of the Ragamuffin. Perhaps he grew up to be a famous rugby player or even a Lord Provost. I was sure he would be somebody, if only in his own rich imagination.

It was more difficult saying goodbye to Aunt Bessie and Uncle Tom who grew weepy at the end. Fancy anyone shedding tears over me. For my part, I had difficulty in

holding in my high spirits and was ready to set out for the
rendezvous with Father long before trysting time. Would
he have received my postcard and remembered to come?
I was in an agony of apprehension as I walked down the
wynd with Aunt Bessie and Uncle Tom, pacing my steps
to theirs and curbing my desire to run ahead.

I hardly dared look when we reached the monument, but
he was there before us, peering under the bonnet of Tin
Lizzie who was making her customary noises, shuddering
and shaking as if struck with the palsy. The relief was so
great I could have rushed forward and kissed him, but of
course that would never have done. He just banged down
the bonnet and said, 'Hop in, lass.' Then, after a word or
two with the old folk, we were off.

I looked back and waved. They seemed a lonely pair
standing there in the street and I began to regret that I
had not been nicer. Oh! but it was great to be free. All
the way home Father ignored me, letting me sit still and
think my own thoughts. I liked that. He whistled 'The
Bonnie Bonnie Hoose o' Airlie' at intervals and roared
'Gee-up' to the motor when it backfired on an incline
near Denholm. But not a word about what was going on at
home or how everyone had missed me. Not that anyone
had, I supposed.

Halfway home Tin Lizzie stuck and I got out to help
with the pushing before being sent to a cottage for a pail
of water to cool the engine. Everything was back to
normal. I felt fine.

The farther we went away from Hawick the more I
tried to straighten out the tangle of impressions the visit
had left on my mind. It had enriched me in many ways.
I had experienced a whole range of new sensations, some I
would never want to repeat again. It was all a muddle, of
course, but the one sure and certain conclusion at which I
arrived was that there was nothing in the world better
than freedom. Nothing!

Forever after I was to dread 'staying with people'. The scar is still there. To this day I find myself going to ridiculous lengths to avoid being boxed-in in someone else's hospitable house, preferring an impersonal hotel where I can come and go unchallenged. Kindness can sometimes kill.

Jessie was plucking a hen in the kitchen and Mother making a roly-poly pudding when I arrived home. They both stopped long enough to say, 'Hullo, you're back,' before continuing with their tasks. I watched Mother spreading rasp jam on the pudding before rolling it up, then turned to Jessie.

'That's not Jenny?' I asked anxiously as she took tufts of feathers from the bird hanging head-down from her lap.

'No, it's just a hen. Get oot ma road an' dinna mak' the feathers flee.'

She had spread sheets of the *Scotsman* on the floor to catch the fluff and feathers as they fell, and was pursing her lips in concentration. Jessie had plucked hundreds of birds in her day: chickens, partridges, pheasants, grouse, ducks and bubblyjocks, and had done her best to teach me, too. But I was slow at the job, always afraid I was hurting the poor feathered creature, stone dead though it was.

It was nice not to be noticed. I just went outside, took to my heels and ran all over the farm with no one pestering me. No Aunt Bessie to say, 'Where are you going, dearie?' No Uncle Tom warning me not to catch cold. No woolly scarf, no mollycoddling. It was wonderful to be my own self again. I sang 'Shall We Gather at the River?' at the pitch of my voice, not because I felt holy but because the rumbustious tune suited my mood.

I did everything as fast as I could. Climbed a haystack, shinned up a tree, swung perilously high on my own swing, rushed to the hill to see if the castle was still there and came home through the wood, listening to the trees. I thought of the Ragamuffin as I fingered the pebble in my pocket and wondered if he had used his scented soap yet.

Jed and Jess came sniffing towards me giving little yelps of recognition. Jock-the-herd greeted me with, 'Man-lassie!' He looked kind of pleased to see me.

'How are you, Jock?'

'Me?'

He was surprised at the question. Jock never thought how he was. He just was. I nearly asked him if he had missed me, but stopped myself in time.

He liked the red and white spotted handkerchief. At least he shook it out and examined it closely before stowing it away in an inside pocket. He seemed surprised that I had survived.

'A week in thon place! A hale week! Were ye no' fair scunnered?'

But by now I was beginning to brag a bit. 'It was rare,' I told him defiantly. 'Rare! I enjoyed myself a treat.'

'Better you than me.' The herd went off, shaking his head, and I realised I was as bad as the Ragamuffin. Telling thumpers.

It was the same when I wrote my thank-you letter to the old folk. There was no way, it seemed, of getting through life without twisting the truth.

'Dear Aunt Bessie and Uncle Tom, How are you? I am all right. My cold's away.'

That was fair enough but I had to say something else and lay it on thick. 'I fairly enjoyed myself in Hawick. It was kind of you to invite me. I hope I'll see you again soon. I am missing you both. Tell everybody I was asking for them.' Everybody being the neighbours we visited and the talking budgie.

It was not much of a letter. I could have written a better one to the Ragamuffin but I had no idea what his address was. The Park, Hawick, Roxburghshire, Scotland, the World. I doubted if it would reach him.

For the rest of the holidays I ran wild, living my own

self-contained life and not caring a button about scratched legs, torn frocks or tangled hair.

I spent whole days in the keep on the hill, not bothering to go back to the farmhouse for meals. I fed myself on books instead, eating up print as I read and re-read *Oliver Twist* or *The Mill on the Floss*. Sometimes when I came back to life I found my feet had fallen asleep and I was all pins and needles. I kept an old skipping-rope in the castle so I could jump myself back into circulation, counting up to a hundred or singing:

> Matthew, Mark, Luke and John.
> Haud the cuddy till I get on . . .

Sometimes I helped Jock with the sheep. I was pleased when he shouted, 'Man-lassie, weir that yowe through the yett.' I was becoming more knowledgeable about rams, tups, hogs, yowes and gimmers. Almost as good, so I hoped, as an extra collie. Or I went off to the fields with the hinds, acting as bondager, and rode back on one of the Clydesdales, clinging to its mane and pretending not to be terrified when the great clumping creature clattered into the steading and made straight for the horse-trough, slobbering and slavering as it slaked its thirst.

I was soon back to my normal state of disarray, tousled and tatty, speaking with a broad Border accent and earning the scorn of my ladylike elder sister who considered me beneath contempt.

'*You!*' she would say distastefully. 'You're not even fit to be a skivvy.'

'I'm going to be a bondager,' I said defiantly, aspiring to higher things.

But she could reduce me to dust with one look, so I kept out of her way as much as possible. If visitors came to tea I hid up a tree and let her take all the praise for her prim manners. She was soon away back to her Edinburgh college, and suddenly it was time for me, too, to spruce myself up, ready for my return to the Grammar School. It was a painful process.

'Ye're as tousy as a tyke,' declared Jessie as she tried to get the rugs out of my hair. 'What'll the folk in Jethart think o' ye?'

'I'm not caring.'

But I cared enough to submit to her ministrations so that I could present a tidy enough appearance at school not to be noticed one way or another. The worst part was wearing stockings and forcing my feet into restricting shoes.

The first person I met going through the school gates was Lucy, the ewe-lamb. Both her parents had accompanied her and were standing waving her goodbye with downcast looks as if she was leaving for the ends of the earth, though they would be back at lunchtime to collect her. She had a new satchel which she proudly showed me, and a wrist watch with a gold band, no less. But I no longer envied her. The silken chains would be too tight for me, though she seemed to thrive on them.

Though we were all 'Jock Tamson's bairns' born under the same Border umbrella, how varied we all were in our characters. As I turned and saw her parents still lingering at the gates for a last look at their pet I was glad to know that Mother was expecting again.

Yet when the English teacher set us the task of writing an essay on How I Spent My Summer Holiday I found myself throwing the hammer once again. The truth was not in me. What a splendid week I had spent in Hawick! The streets, the shops, the people, the talking budgie, the cosy little house, the kindness of Aunt Bessie and Uncle Tom. All was exaggerated, but no mention of the Ragamuffin. I had enjoyed every moment of it; my only regret was that one week had been too short.

The teacher gave me full marks and I was forced for my sins to stand in front of the class to read out my effusion.

Serve me right!

7. Snow and Storms

The first time I made the surprising discovery that my parents were fond of me, in a sort of a way, was when I got lost in a snowstorm. I was glad I did not die or I would never have known.

It made me wonder, though, why folk kept their warm hearts so well-hidden, only showing their real feelings in moments of stress. Sometimes never at all. Borderers were seldom blate (Jessie's word for bashful) when it came to plain speaking, expressing downright opinions and giving folk their characters. Yet their tongues were tied in knots when voicing their deepest emotions. Any form of endearment stuck in their thrapples. How could one crack such hard shells?

How different from the characters in story-books who dear-ed and darling-ed each other on every page, but that, of course, was fiction. Tenderness and affection were maybe not meant for real life. Still, I thought it a pity that the hinds and their wives never seemed to give each other a glance, let alone a fond one. Even when they were courting they did not once mention the word love. No doubt it was there, deep down, but why keep it hidden? Was it such a shameful thing to do as the bible said and love one another?

I was used to it, so I grew a shell like everyone else, but I always felt there was something missing. Many a time I had the urge to throw my arms round Jessie's neck – or the herd's – and express my affection for them. I could do it to a calf or a pet lamb but never to a human being.

It was something inside me that must be curbed. Like the desire to shout 'Shut up!' to the minister when he went on too long with his dreary sermon. Thou shalt not!

It never once entered my head that anyone could love me. Except perhaps Aunt Bessie and Uncle Tom, and a little of that went a long way. At home I had the feeling I was in everyone's way, so I tried to make myself as invisible as Maister Naebody. In fact, I was a kind of *Miss* Nobody, coming and going without anyone paying any particular attention to me. 'Stand on your ain feet, lassie,' Jessie used to advise me, so I stood on them. There was no one to lean on, anyway, especially on that dreadful day when I got stuck in the snow.

The storm came on suddenly just as I was jumping down from the school bus at the crossroads outside Mary-Ann's cottage. If I had known what was in store for me I would have stayed there and begged Mary-Ann for shelter. She would have welcomed me, I felt sure, for she used to talk to me as if I were one of her hens, and often fed me with a jeelly-piece to help me on my way. Once she even offered me a handful of corn from her apron pocket.

Looking after her feathered friends was Mary-Ann's chief preoccupation. She treated them like children, fussing over them as if she herself was a mother hen. She clucked at them and knew each one by name. Maggie, Mrs Broon,

Wee Rascal, Banty, His Nibs, and the rest. According to her, they each had their own personality.

'Just like folk. See Mrs Broon! She's no' speakin' to onybody. Puir thing, she's in the pouk. Lost a' her feathers. Mebbe I'd better tak' her into the hoose. She likes sittin' on the kitchen rug.'

Later, I wished I had had the sense to sit there, too, instead of pressing on through the swirling snow.

'Watch yoursel', wee ane!' Black Sandy called to me as he turned the bus. 'We're in for a beezer o' a storm. Awa' hame at the toot. Onward Christian Soldiers!' And off he went, skidding on the icy road.

It crackled under my feet as I walked away from Mary-Ann's reminding me of the poem Miss Paleface had been teaching us at school. About the Ancient Mariner.

> The ice was here, the ice was there,
> The ice was all around;
> It cracked and growled, and roared and howled,
> Like noises in a swound.

At first it was beautiful. The feathery flakes came flying thick and fast from the sky, settling on the trees and transforming the grey countryside into what those who knew little about snowstorms would call a white wonderland. But I had been snowed in too often to waste time extolling its beauty. Darkness had fallen early, the wind was rising, the icy air growing colder. It whipped the snow into swirls, stinging against my cheeks and freezing on my hair. I had to keep blinking my eyelids to free my lashes from the flakes.

By the time I reached the farm roadend I could scarcely see a step in front of me, the air was so thick with snow-flakes. The ground by now was covered and every land-mark obliterated. Was I turning in at the right roadend or had I wandered by mistake into a field? I had to turn my back now and again from the force of the storm so that I could regain my breath, hoping that soon I might see the lights from the hinds' cottage windows and know that I was on home ground, but there was no lamplit glow to be seen, no sound except the wail of the wind. I seemed to be walking aimlessly in circles and getting nowhere.

Up till now I had felt a certain sense of adventure – even elation – seeing myself as a heroine overcoming all odds. After all, snow was my element. My first view of the world had been a white one, for I was born in a storm, shut in for the first six weeks of my life, and when at last I was carried outside the snow-wreaths were still there, higher than the hedgerows. Since then I had plodded through drifts many a time and experienced all the dis-comforts of being storm-stayed. But never before had I felt so overpowered by the angry elements, raging against me like fiends.

I tried to stem the rising feeling of panic. Be sensible! Think! If I was in a field surely there must be a dyke nearby. If I could reach it I might be able to find my bearings, or at least cower behind it from the force of the driving snow, but every step I took led me nowhere. By now I was finding it more difficult to keep my feet, and as I stumbled and fell, I realised I was in real danger.

Old tales came flooding back to my mind of tramps found frozen to death in the snow. Never mind Lucy Gray; *she* was only in a poem. These had been flesh-and-blood beings who had lost their lives in sudden storms like this. If it had happened to them it could happen to me.

I wondered if anyone at home had noticed I was missing or would they all be too engrossed in their own affairs? At least, if I was finally found frozen stiff like the tramps all my sins would be forgiven and forgotten. It was some consolation but not much.

A great desire came over me to lie still in the soft snow-bed into which I had fallen. If I snuggled down and went to sleep – a last sleep – all my worries would be over. For a second I drowsed off, before pulling myself up sharply. 'Get up, lassie,' I seemed to hear Jessie saying. 'Pit your best fit forrit.'

Which foot was my best. I had little feeling in either. By now I had lost my gloves and my fingers were dead. But through thick and thin I clung to my school satchel, knowing it contained not only my lesson-books and a library book – *Lorna Doone* – which must be returned in due course to Miss Paleface if I survived, but also some messages I had been asked to collect from the shops in Jedburgh that day. Tobacco for one of the hinds, darning-wool, safety-pins, shoe-polish and a pair of black boot-laces. Nothing heavy, luckily, or of great import, yet I had been entrusted with the money to buy them. Tam would be lost with an empty pipe, and frozen tobacco was better than none.

Sometimes I floundered in a snow-filled ditch. Was it the one near home where the red rowans grew and the little barberry bushes? Or was I maybe miles away from the farmhouse on someone else's land? Once when I fell I felt something stirring beside me, alive and warm. A sheep. If I could have seen the markings on its fleece, I would have known if it was one of ours. Perhaps I had helped to stamp the initials on its back at clipping-time when the herds shouted 'Buist!' and I ran to dip the branding-iron into the tar-pot. Would I ever hear that sound again?

The creature seemed content enough to lie there burrowed under the snow. Perhaps it would survive. I had heard Jock tell of digging sheep out alive weeks after being lost in a storm. If I lay beside it maybe I could survive, too, but I was not a sheep. No woolly covering or inner layers of fat to preserve me from the bitter cold. Instinct urged me to struggle to my feet and keep going.

Every step grew more difficult. My legs ached, my eyes smarted, my face had lost all feeling and my hair hung heavily over my shoulders, frozen into stiff plaits of ice which bumped against my back, adding to my burden. There seemed little point in going on. I had tried, and now I must give in.

The next time I stumbled I lay where I fell in a mound of snow, soft and comfortable as a feather-bed. Soon I would have a white counterpane to cover me and all my troubles would be over. I began to say my bedtime prayer, the last I would ever repeat.

> Now I lay me down to sleep,
> I pray the Lord my soul to keep,
> If I should die before I wake . . .

Was that a Willy-Wisp dancing before my eyes?

I was hearing noises. In this world or the next? A bobbing light appeared to be advancing towards me and I could hear somebody or something prodding through the snow. Jock-the-herd with his crook. Then I heard Father's voice and Jock shouting as he laid down his lantern. 'She's here! I've got her! Man-lassie . . .'

The lost sheep had been found.

I remember the herd hoisting me up from the ground and slinging me over his shoulders like a sack of corn. I was still clutching my school satchel and Father had a job to prise it from my frozen fingers. On the way home the feeling that I had caused such a lot of trouble overcame everything else, even that my ordeal was past.

'I'm awful sorry,' I murmured, bobbing against Jock's broad back.

'It's all right, lass,' my father said kindly, walking beside us with the lantern. 'You're safe, that's all that matters.'

Mother, too, was all softness and kindness when I was carried into the lamplit kitchen. Her eyes were red as if she had been crying. For me?

The next thing I remember was being in bed. Warm

blankets, a hot pig, a feeling of great comfort, and a lump in my throat as I thought of everyone's kindness.

Now I lay me down to sleep . . .

In the morning, of course, it was all different. I was no longer a heroine and nobody took much notice of me. Except Jessie who gave me a sound scolding.

'Could ye no' hae used your rummlegumption an' stopped at Mary-Ann's?'

Back to normal.

All the same, the memory lingered on. The warm feeling was there, and I decided to repay everybody by being nicer to them in future. But that, too, soon wore off. Yet I now knew for sure that I was not just a nobody in the family. I counted for *something*. ·

It must have been about this time that I made another surprising discovery. Jessie was not quite perfect.

It all began with the lambing-man. Every winter, the Boss, my father, hired an extra help to take the burden off Jock-the-herd's overloaded shoulders when the sheep began to lamb. The two men took turn about on night-duty, making the bothy up at the lambing-shed their headquarters. There was a trestle bed there and a fire where they could heat milk for the motherless lambs and brew their own tea. A row of sinister-looking bottles containing medicine for sick sheep stood on a dusty shelf. In a way, it was like a clinic for expectant mothers.

Nearby were the bields which the herd had built to shelter the more difficult cases brought in from the ends of the farm; but mostly the mothers gave birth out in the open, often at dead of night and in the wildest weather. It was a miracle how the lambs survived and so soon grew sturdy enough to fend for themselves. Suddenly plunged into an icy-cold world, up on their feet from the moment they were born, finding instant sustenance from their mothers, and often a helping hand from the herd or the lambing-man.

I remember a succession of such lambing-men but none more clearly than Erchie, the reason being the bothy roof had gone on fire – it was built of thatch and went up in a spectacular blaze – and Erchie was forced to stay off and on in the farmhouse, while I was relegated, as usual, to sleep with Liz-Ann, the servant-girl whom Jessie called the Cairthorse.

Liz-Ann was a great snorer, and so was Erchie for I could hear him through the wall ascending and descending the scales before reaching a crescendo and fading away into nothing as if he had died. I waited apprehensively for the symphony to restart. Sometimes he varied it with a loud whistle which made my blood curdle, especially if I was on the verge of falling asleep myself; and now and again Liz-Ann would grow restless and lash out at me with her feet, or flail her arms and hit me on the face. Often I was black and blue in the morning, but judging from the thuds and creaks from next door I would sooner have shared her bed than Erchie's.

All the same, I quite liked him. Not so Jessie.

It was like Dr Fell, the reason why she could not tell. He was an inoffensive enough big soul, with tufts of sandy hair growing straight up from his head, false teeth which clicked when he spoke, and a great desire to please but he could not please Jessie. Everything he said or did annoyed her. The way he saucered his tea, ate his food with his knife, sat with his stockinged soles on the kitchen fender, whistled endlessly under his breath.

'Can ye no' haud your wheesht?' she would say in an exasperated voice, rounding on him in a fury. 'I'm fair deived wi' "The Laird o' Cockpen".'

'Richt!' said Erchie placidly. 'I'll gie ye "Auld Lang Syne" insteed.'

I enjoyed listening to them catter-battering, like a pair of music-hall comics on the stage, though in Jessie's case it was in deadly earnest. According to her, Erchie was responsible for all the evils of mankind. Red spots of anger would appear on her cheeks as she ranted at him, but all her abuse seemed to bounce off his back. Try as she would – and she tried – she could not find a vulnerable spot.

'Dodsakes, Jessie,' he would say mildly, 'ye've got a tongue that wad clip cloots.'

'Dinna Jessie me!'

It was no longer Mr Nobody who caused all the trouble in the household. It was Erchie who lost the scissors, broke cups, upset the milk-jug and left dirty marks on the kitchen floor. No use trying to defend him, Jessie knew better. He was even accused of stealing the clothes-line when it went missing.

'He did not,' I would say in his defence.

'Did sot!'

When it turned up under the kitchen table she was convinced Erchie had hidden it there deliberately to annoy her. It became an obsession with her, so much so that Erchie used to fling his skippet-bunnet into the kitchen before daring to set foot in it himself. They never actually came to blows, only verbal ones, though Jessie often warned him, 'I'll skelp your lugs if ye dinna get oot ma road.'

Jock-the-herd had no complaints about Erchie's work. 'He's guid wi' the lambs,' and that was all that mattered to Jock.

But not to Jessie.

One day the clash of personalities reached its climax. I came down that morning to find Jessie rampaging about the place with the red danger-signals in her cheeks. The Cairthorse was cowering in the back-kitchen and Erchie sitting supping his porridge at the table, dipping his spoon first into a bowl of creamy milk at the side and then into the porridge plate, time and about.

'Impidence!' snorted Jessie, breathing fire as she lifted

the porridge pot and loomed over him as if about to
spear him with the spirtle.

'What's up?' I enquired.

'Up! It's *him*. Canna ca' ma kitchen ma ain. Interferin'
busy-body, that's him.'

Erchie continued to sup his porridge. Between mouthfuls
he explained. 'There was naebody aboot when I cam'
doon, so I just made the porridge.' A kindly enough
gesture, I thought.

'It's fou o' knots,' grumped Jessie, dumping the pot
on the table and giving the contents a vigorous stir.

''Tis not,' said Erchie.

''Tis sot!'

They were like a couple of squabbling bairns. It was no
use acting as intermediary, so I sat down at the table and
waited for Jessie to dish out my helping of porridge. She
gave an angry twist to the pot and the next moment it
turned on its side, spilling out a stream of boiling-hot
porridge. Most of it landed on the unfortunate Erchie's
hand. He gave a howl of pain and sprang to his feet, while
Jessie said crossly, 'See what ye've dune noo! Cowped
the pot!'

'I did not,' said Erchie, clicking his false teeth.

'Did sot!'

'Oh, Jessie!' I protested, dumbfounded.

'Haud your tongue!' she snapped at me, and began to
clear up the mess on the table while Erchie rushed through
to the back-kitchen, almost knocking over the Cairthorse,
to run the cold water over his scalded hand, after which
with a great display of dignity he went out of the house,
not looking at Jessie or saying another word.

'Poor soul, he hasn't finished his breakfast,' I began,
then after a look at Jessie's face decided it would be more
prudent to bite my tongue. Fancy her telling such a black
lie! It astounded me to discover that Jessie, of all people,
had feet of clay.

All that day she went about tight-lipped. Now and again she thumped herself angrily on the stomach. I knew the signs.

'Is anything wrong, Jessie?' I ventured to ask, when I saw her sipping a cup of hot water.

'I've got the bile. Keep oot ma road.'

So I kept out of her road. So did the lambing-man. It was his turn on night-duty, using the bothy as his head-quarters, therefore it was not till next day that we heard him stamping the snow off his boots before flinging his hat into the kitchen.

'How's your hand?' I asked him when he came in.

'Fine!'

He tried to hide it behind his back but not before I had seen that it looked raw and blistered. Jessie had noticed it, too. She said nothing but went to the dresser and rummaged in one of the drawers till she found a roll of bandages.

'Sit doon,' she ordered Erchie. 'Haud oot your hand.'

Erchie sat down and meekly allowed himself to be bandaged. No words passed between them, but I sensed it was Jessie's way of saying she was sorry.

There was no truce, though I was surprised that night to see her darning a pair of the lambing-man's socks. But soon the two of them were argy-bargying as before, each trying to score points off the other.

'Did not!'

'Did sot!'

And suddenly I realised it was a kind of game which they both enjoyed playing. Like peevers, kick-the-can, or cuddy-loup-the-dyke. Grown-ups were no different from children. No more flawless. So maybe my own imperfections did not matter all that much. I was not disillusioned with Jessie. Indeed, I liked her better now that I found she had human failings. Perfection is not a lovable quality. She seemed more like me now, though, of course, miles above me in strength of character.

As for Erchie he just went away when the lambing-season was over, still clicking his false teeth and whistling 'The Laird o' Cockpen' under his breath.

'Guid riddance!' grunted Jessie as he disappeared down the road.

All the same, I felt she would miss him.

8. Dreams and Daydreamers

Father's funny-bone worked overtime. Asleep or awake, he always seemed to be involved in some comic incident.

Sometimes I could hear great guffaws of laughter coming from the work-stable and guessed that the Boss had dropped in for a word with the men at lowsing-time while they were feeding and curry-combing the workhorses. He was not one for giving orders, only for suggesting what work might be done about the farm next day, in such a way that the hinds seemed to have made the decisions themselves. Certainly they liked his company and looked forward to his visits.

The Boss could always find something funny to relate even in the simplest daily happening, and things had a way of happening to him. Like the day his lum hat walked across the floor, before his very eyes, with the cat underneath it. It was not so much the happenings, as the way Father told them. He was a born raconteur. No one could ever be dull in his company.

If he was in the mood.

At times he could be as withdrawn as any hermit, shutting himself up in the greenhouse, his refuge from the outside world. Here he kept a private collection of odds and ends. Song-sheets, a jew's harp, seed catalogues, unanswered letters and frayed copies of the Jethart Squeaker. Often I caught sight of him through the glass of the greenhouse, watering his seedlings, sitting on an upturned tub, puzzling over an account book, playing the jew's harp, or just sitting there. But I never watched for long. There was no Do Not Disturb notice on the door, but we all knew that if the Boss was in his hidey-hole the best thing to do was ignore him.

There was little enough privacy in such a stirring household where it was difficult for any of us to find a private corner of our own. Lucky me, with my castle on the hill.

Father often went to ground when any awkward decision had to be made. He was not one for facing up to trouble or giving someone a telling-off. In any family squabble he was inclined to walk out of earshot or say, if asked to act as arbiter, 'Leave it to your mother.' In the greenhouse he was safe. Fantasy was pleasanter than facts.

More often the Boss was in a gregarious mood. He loved company, and when visitors arrived instantly became a performer. I, for one, could have listened to him till the cows came home, especially if he was recounting his dreams. Asleep, father had adventures even funnier than his waking ones.

People who record their dreams are mostly as boring as those who give chapter and verse about how they spent every single day of their holidays.

'On the Monday it rained in the morning. No, I'm wrong, that was Tuesday. On Monday the sun was shining so we walked down to the beach to look at the sea. Then in the afternoon . . .'

Similarly with dreamers. 'I must tell you about a funny dream I had last night.' *Why* must they?

Jessie cured me. I had subjected her to a rambling tale of how I flew through the air in the middle of the night and landed upside-down on the steeple clock in Jedburgh. She was not impressed.

'Keep your dreams to yoursel', wumman, or ye'll get put awa'.'

'Where?'

'In the daft-hoose.'

'Oh!' It was a sobering thought. 'Do you never dream, Jessie?'

'Me? I've got mair to do wi' ma time.'

'But you've nothing to do with your time when you're asleep.'

'I have sot! I'm ower busy sleepin'.'

Her brother, the herd, on the other hand, once admitted he sometimes had nightmares.

'What about, Jock?'

'Aboot black-faced sheep. Thoosands o' them, chasin' me ower a precipice.'

'Mercy me! What happens?'

'Nae idea. I aye wake up in time.'

Most of the dreams I heard about had no beginning, middle and end. Except Father's, and they lost nothing in the telling. I sometimes wondered if he was making them up, but maybe they were all as true as true.

He was a great one, Father, for meeting royalty in the middle of the night.

'Guess who I met last night.' Pause for effect. 'King George.'

'Goodness gracious! What was he doing?'

'Riding up the road on your bicycle.'

'The boneshaker! Never!' No wonder I was astounded at the thought of royalty riding my old rattletrap which I could hardly ride myself now that its handlebars were twisted and so many of its spokes missing. 'How did he manage?'

'He fell off,' said Father, which did not surprise me, 'and so did his crown, right in the middle of a puddle.'

'Mercy me! what did he say?'

'A bad word.'

'What?'

Father hesitated and then said, 'Dammit!'

'Oh!' Fancy the king saying a word like that, even in a dream. 'Did you say anything?'

'Yes, I said Hullo, George.'

'George! Did you not say Your Majesty?'

'Never thought of it. I asked him where Mary was.'

'Queen Mary!'

'Ay! So George said she was riding Flora up the road, wearing her coronation robes. She was right cross when she saw the king lying there. She called him a silly sumph and told him to get up and put his crown back on his head or he'd get what-for. So George said another bad word and got up . . . '

It was all so silly and yet so feasible. On and on went the story, no detail left out, till I could see King George and Queen Mary as plain as porridge in the kitchen (always with crowns on their heads), George in stockinged soles making toast at the fire while Mary tied an apron round her coronation robes and said, 'I'll just go out to milk the kye. Have a boiled egg ready for me, George, when I come back . . . '

Sometimes the tables were turned and it was Father who found himself in Buckingham Palace, dressed in his lum hat and long johns, with Queen Mary pipe-claying the doorstep – still, of course, with her crown on her head – and asking, 'Would you care for a kipper to your tea. Or a clooty-dumpling?'

Father's dreams were not always confined to night-time. I remember the day he fell asleep in church during the long sermon and began to roar with laughter until mother dunted him awake.

He was not the only one to doze off. Religion seemed to have a soporific effect on the congregation, many of whom had walked miles across country after a hard week's work. Now that they were settled down in their pews, uncomfortable though the hard seats were, who could blame them for sinking into blissful oblivion? Surely God would give them full marks for being present in the flesh though absent in spirit.

I was not much of a sleeper myself even in bed at night, so as I sucked my pandrop, I was able to observe the drowsy worshippers' efforts to stay awake. I watched Jock-the-herd nodding in the pew across the way, his head sinking lower and lower on his chest, while his sisters Jessie and Joo-anne sat bolt upright beside him, eyes fixed unblinkingly on the pulpit. I had a feeling they, too, were asleep even though their eyes were open, for sometimes they gave convulsive jerks or let out soulful sighs.

There were many strange sounds to be heard all round me, apart from the minister's monotonous voice. Suppressed snores, grunts, groans and wheezes. It was a blessing Erchie, the lambing-man, did not come to the kirk or he would have raised the roof. Big Bob sometimes took a coughing-fit just to pass the time and in the hope that someone would hand him a sweetie to clear his throat. Old Miss Eliot in the back pew gave in before the minister had finished 'Firstly' and laid her head on the book-board in front of her as if it were a pillow. I sometimes wished His Reverence would follow suit in the pulpit but he seemed to be the only one enjoying his own performance.

Up in the gallery the laird and his lot from the Big Hoose had more comfortable dreams on their cushioned seats. Red plush. When Sir J. M. Barrie was with them the wee man disappeared completely from sight for the duration of the sermon and I wondered if he was lying stretched out or just sitting hunched up like Humpty Dumpty. I wondered, too (having nothing else to do) if there were kirk mice up there or if it was too grand a place for them.

I was dying to know what had made father laugh. He told us on the way home. It was an appropriate dream for the occasion.

'All about Moses,' Father said, his eyes crinkling with laughter as he recalled the scene. 'Playing rugby for Jedforest, belting down the field to score a try when a big fella from Hawick tackled him and tore off his breeks.'

'Gracious! What happened?'

Father shook his head. 'Your mother woke me when Moses was being carried off on a stretcher, poor soul. I doubt he had broken more than his commandments.'

Looking back, I can see that my father was no ordinary man. I felt it at the time, though I thought it was maybe only a child's view of someone I admired, but now that I have a clearer picture of him I am more sure of it. I was always bursting with pride when I heard his praises being sung. I felt no modesty about it. 'Yes! isn't he great?' I agreed.

The sad thing was, I could never say it to his face.

Fair enough for Father to dream while he was asleep. My trouble was that I daydreamed. It led me into many a pickle.

Jessie sometimes shook me by the shoulders to bring me back to reality and said sharply, 'Stop it, lassie. Ye're awa' in a dwam again. What are ye thinkin' aboot?'

I would never tell. Daytime dreams were private. They were not funny, like Father's. Mine were full of fantasy, mainly with me as heroine. The opposite from real life. I was brave, beautiful, beloved by everyone. I had the magic touch and could cure all ills. People flocked from far and near to beg for my help. I was showered with gifts. Precious jewels, pearls, rubies, sacks of gold.

Statues were built in my honour, streets named after me. I was in the history books like Cleopatra.

The great thing about daydreaming was it helped to take the tedium out of a dull task. Drying the dishes or doing the kirning. The churning. Or it could carry me into oblivion over a rough road. On the way to the village school, for example. The trouble was it sometimes carried me too far.

I can remember the time I went away past Edgerston, on and on, up towards the Carter Bar, daydreaming my way to the Cheviots instead of turning in at the school gate. I remember it specially because it was the day Bella at the post office had a new line in 'confectionary'. Toffee apples. They were new to me and as I was in funds after purchasing a jotter I spent my remaining halfpenny on the strange sweetmeat.

'What do I do with it?' I asked, holding it awkwardly in my hand by its wooden stalk.

'Sook it, lassie, or chowe it,' Bella told me. 'Use your heid.'

I used my teeth instead. The coating of toffee was sweet and crackly. In contrast the apple inside tasted sour. Still, I was not going to throw it away after spending all that money on it. So I chewed my way up the road past the Camptown cottages, through the Dark Woods and on towards the Manse and the school.

In order to take my mind off the sourness I embarked on one of my favourite fantasies. Like King Midas, everything I touched turned to gold. Hedges, fences, trees, flowers, weeds, even the stone I was kicking up the road. Mine was a revised version of the classic story. I doubt if I had even heard of Midas at that time in my life. So I let my imagination roam and transformed the whole countryside into a realm of gold, unaware that I had long passed the school gate.

With such wealth at my command how was I going

to spend it? *That* kept me going for a long stretch of steep road. A golden cradle for the baby, bracelets and rings for my mother, a splendid brand-new greenhouse for father, new bicycles for the hinds and silken dresses for their wives.

I puzzled for ages about Jock-the-herd. Would he like a gold crook or a new bowler hat to wear to the kirk? And what about Jessie? It would have to be something practical, like carbolic soap or safety-pins, but I would sooner have given her pure gold earrings, though I knew she would never have worn them.

Filling in all these details kept me fully occupied, little realising where my feet were carrying me till I heard a sudden shout which brought me back to earth with a bump. All the gold faded away in a flash and I was left with nothing but the wooden stick of my toffee-apple.

'Daursay, lassie, what are ye daein' awa' up here? Ye're miles past the schule.'

It was Auld Chuckie-Stanes, the roadman, chipping away at a heap of stones and shaking his head at me. 'Ye'd better turn aboot an' rin for't.'

I turned and ran like a hare down the road, but not fast enough, of course. The class had long been assembled when I slunk in and tried to reach my desk unnoticed. Auld Baldy-Heid was writing a sum on the blackboard, but he had eyes in the back of his head.

'And where d'you think you've been, miss,' he thundered, addressing the blackboard though his venom was directed at me.

'P-please, s-sir . . . ' What was the use of telling him I had been away in a golden wonderland? Better just to say I was late, which was obvious enough, and take the consequences. Big Bob would have done better. He had a hoard of more or less feasible excuses which sometimes fooled the teacher. 'Please, sir, the coo was calving.' 'I had to rin a message for ma granny. She canna rin hersel', wi' her bad leg.' 'Please sir, ma mither had to mend ma troosers.'

I tried my hardest not to daydream in the classroom but I did not alway succeed. Sometimes I came to my senses to discover Auld Baldy-Heid looming over me like the wrath of God.

'Did you hear what I said, girl? Answer me.'

'Yessir. I mean, no sir.'

I had to take a firmer grip on myself when I went to the Grammar School, though in a way it was easier there. With so many comings and goings from one classroom to another, and all the different subjects to learn, I was forced to concentrate on immediate matters. It was only in the Latin class that I could really let go. Anything to escape from the subject.

Mr Archie-Bald, the rector, took the class himself in his own room, and there I sat with some of the boys from my own class, also reluctantly taking this extra subject. Why we never knew. The only compensation was that Dafty left us to our own devices for long periods while he went into a dwam, and I was able to follow suit, but I had to keep a wary eye on the irascible wee man for there was no knowing when he would suddenly come back to earth and bawl, 'Get up on your feet, man, and read that first paragraph.' He called me man along with the boys, but that was the least of my troubles.

During his long withdrawn silences while he sat hunched up at his desk, I could escape, too. The boys were up to various ploys below their desks. Sometimes they made inky pellets with blotting paper and fired them at each other – or me – with their rulers, and now and again Miss Crichton or one of the other teachers would bring in a juvenile delinquent to be punished. Or the Janny would knock at the door to announce that a laddie had went and broke a windy. But apart from these interruptions there were long spells when I could let my imagination roam.

It was during these daytime dreams that I made my parents proud of me.

'Yes, that's our daughter. Isn't she wonderful?'

I saved people from drowning, rescued them from burning buildings, risked life and limb by climbing a high tower to bring down a stranded child. Or I stepped on to the stage at the last moment to take over a prima donna's part, with outstanding success, of course. My photograph was in all the papers, not just the Jethart Squeaker. It was not pride in myself that mattered. The only thing I cared about was that Father and Mother were there to revel in my success.

I used to wonder what went on in Dafty's head when he was missing from the real world. What were his fantasies? Far removed from the Grammar School, I felt sure. Sometimes he nodded his head and gave a wry smile, and occasionally he shook hands with himself as if saying, 'Well done, boy!' But more often his brow darkened and he appeared to be engaged in an angry argument. It would not have surprised me if he had opened his desk, brought out the tawse and walloped his unseen opponent.

It would have been interesting, I thought, to listen in to what went on privately in everyone's head, not that they could be a patch on Father's dreams.

When he started off with, 'Guess where I was last night,' I knew we were in for a treat.

'The moon?'

'No.'

'Where, then?'

'Davy Jones's locker.'

'At the bottom of the sea! Mercy me! what were you doing there?'

'Driving the motor,' said Father. 'I met Jonah and the whale.' He would! 'And d'you know what? Jonah was the spitting image of Jock-the-herd. I gave him a lift home . . .'

9. Facts and Fancies

'Bairns should be seen and not heard.'

How often this was said to me in my childhood; too often.

Speak when you're spoken to. Keep your opinions to yourself. Who are you, anyway, to have opinions? Do as you're told. Be obedient. Grown-ups know best. Their word was law, by the mere fact that they were older and therefore wiser. But were they?

I had begun to have my doubts and was looking at them more critically, making my own judgements, seeing their mistakes, finding their flaws. But though they were quick enough to point out my failings I would never have dared criticise theirs. I would instantly have been banished to the garret for being cheeky. There was little justice, it seemed, for the young.

Yet everyone has a need to look up to a higher being. In my case (apart from Jessie) it was a teacher at the Grammar School. The science master.

It was a pity science was one of my worst subjects, for I longed beyond anything to shine in his sight, but he had given me up as hopeless. He told me so many a time, when I came to grief with a Bunsen burner or spilt mercury on the floor. 'Oh you! You're hopeless!' Yet even that sounded like music in my ears and the fact that he had taken any notice of me at all made my heart thump. I used to dream of rescuing him from disasters or bringing off such a splendid experiment that he would say, 'Well done! You're not so hopeless, after all. My favourite pupil.' But it was only fantasy.

It was not his looks that attracted me. He was a small tubby dumpling of a man, with duplicated chins and waistcoat buttons that kept popping from their moorings. Mr Smith was his name. Fatty, the boys called him behind his back. They drew cruel caricatures of him on the blackboard, with a great distended belly, like a butter-ball, but I rubbed them out, when I could, to save hurting his feelings. I never thought of him as Fatty.

The reason I liked him so much, I think, was because of his kindly ways. Even though I was such a dolt he always opened the door for me in a gentlemanly manner (he did it for all the girls) and took the trouble to bandage my bleeding fingers when I cut them on a test tube. 'Just sit still and don't bother with the rest of the lesson. You're hopeless.'

In return I had a great desire to mother him, to sew on his buttons, mend his frayed cuffs, and shield him from the thoughtless pranks of the boys. He looked hurt and bewildered when the chalk was hidden or a simple experiment ended in a smelly explosion. His vulnerability somehow appealed to me and I wanted to protect him from all trials and tribulations. Particularly from Archie-Bald, the rector, who had a habit of sneaking into the science room when we were in the midst of an uproar. Mr Smith's face crumpled up as if he was about to cry and his stammered excuses sounded so futile that I longed to rush to his rescue.

'It was not Mr Smith's fault. He's perfect. It was the boys who did it.'

One day while I was daydreaming in the playground one of the bigger boys in my class kicked a football in my direction – his way of attracting my attention – and yelled out, 'Fatty wants you.'

'Wh-what?'

I was winded both by the football and by Willy's surprising statement. Surely he must be pulling my leg. But he repeated it.

'Fatty wants you. Get a move on; kick the ball back.'

I gave the ball the best kick I could and went off to the science room in a great state of turmoil. What on earth could Mr Smith be wanting with me? To sew on his buttons, or confess his undying admiration for a hopeless pupil? Hardly likely.

I tapped tentatively at the door. Through the glass pane I could see Mr Smith poring over a large sheet of paper, puzzling his brows and making marks here and there. Was he working out a new experiment, or writing me a love-letter?

I had to tap several times before he said 'Come in'. He turned and stared at me as if he had never set eyes on me before. 'Oh yes, you! I want you to be a witch.'

'Yessir,' I replied with blind obedience. Anything he asked. I was willing to get down on all-fours and hop round the room like a frog, if that was what he desired. But how to turn myself into a witch? Maybe I should go and look for one of the Janny's broomsticks.

'I'll need three of you,' said Mr Smith, still studying his paper.

That sounded a bit more difficult. There was only one of me.

'Get two of the other girls in your class. I expect you

can easily get yourselves dressed up as witches. You know, black cloaks and peaked hats. Oh! and you'll need a cauldron.'

'Yessir.' Then I took a deep breath and asked, 'Please sir, what's it for, sir?'

'For?' Mr Smith looked at me as if I was an idiot. 'For the procession, of course.'

It was the first I had heard of the procession but not the last. Only for Mr Smith would I have gone through all the indignities of my first, and only, appearance in the streets of Jedburgh, crouched on a tumbril drawn by a belching horse plodding its way towards the ramparts where the Provost and other dignitaries were assembled to see us pass by.

We were not the only ones. There were drays full of elves, cartloads of Ancient Britons clad in sheepskins and gooseflesh, Robin Hood and his Merry Men, Mary Queen of Scots – a spotty-faced girl from one of the upper classes – and her four Maries, a Nativity Scene complete with a flaxen-haired doll in a cradle, and the entire Jedforest Rugby team marching at the tail end. The town brass band headed the procession and played their way through their repertoire from 'See The Conquering Hero Come' to 'Abide With Me'. They were loud, if nothing else.

I have no recollection of what the occasion was supposed to spotlight or why it had fallen to Mr Smith's lot to organise it, but at least it was unforgettable for one thing. The rain.

Never can there have been a wetter day since the Flood, apart maybe from the one mentioned in the Squeaker fifty years ago. It teemed in torrents, drenching us all to the skin. The elves were soaked through to their chemises, the Ancient Britons tried to shelter their bare knees with mackintoshes, even the Holy Child was awash in the cradle. As for the witches, our peaked hats gave way in the middle of the High Street and sagged over our foreheads, sending rivulets of rain running down our noses.

The only bright spot for me was that Mr Smith was riding the baker's horse by our side, togged up as some sort of cavalier in a green velvet suit, which had silver buttons on the jacket at the start of the procession but none at the end. Poor soul, he kept looking up at the sky as if pleading with God to stop His nonsense, but the higher he looked the more it rained.

We were all coughing and sneezing for weeks after, but at least we got our names and a smudged photograph in the Squeaker. And that was the end of my career as a witch.

It was Father, of course, who was the performer in the family, in great demand at local concerts and soirées where he went down a treat. How proud I was when the audience dunted their feet on the floor, clapped their hands and shouted 'Encore!' It was great basking in his glory. I would sooner have heard him being praised than received an accolade myself.

We were fifty or more miles away from real theatres: Newcastle on the one side, Edinburgh on the other, so there was no chance of seeing stage plays other than the amateur efforts got up by Father. The local performers were always themselves no matter how they were dressed up or who they were supposed to represent in the play. It was only Father who put some fervour into his part, disguising both himself and his voice, though, of course, we knew fine who he was.

'Dodsakes! if I hadna kent that was the Boss I'd never hae recognised him,' one of the hinds said, watching father strutting about the stage, brandishing a bread-knife and dressed as a burglar. I recognised the bread-knife, too. It was the one we kept in the kitchen-table drawer.

My first real glimpse of the theatre came when it was announced that Mr Samuel Somebody, a real live actor, was coming to Southdean, a village three or four miles away, to give a one-man show. No one was quite sure what that was, except that it would be a change from a whist drive, so everyone within reach wended their way to the little hall where the performance was to take place and sat on hard benches staring at the empty platform. Presently a middle-aged man with a club foot came limping forward, and from then on the small stage was crowded.

Never had I seen so many characters, all from Dickens, gathered together as clearly as if they were there in the flesh. I knew some of them already from my reading. Oliver Twist begging for more porridge, Mr Micawber waiting for something to turn up, Mr Pickwick skating on the ice. Fagin teaching his boys how to pick pockets, Little Nell on her deathbed, the unctious Uriah Heep. They were all *there*, conjured out of the air by the actor. I sat mouse-still, hardly daring to draw breath in case I missed a word, completely carried away.

I have no idea what the rest of the audience made of it, but to me it was magic. At the end when the actor limped forward and bowed I could not believe he was only one man. It took ages for me to come down to earth. I could not get over the fact that as soon as we were outside the neighbours began to speak about ordinary things like how the turnips were coming on and when the clipping would start.

I thought about it for a long time afterwards, marvelling not only at the cleverness of the actor but at the genius of the writer who had first created the characters out of his head. It gave me an added incentive to keep on trying to put words on paper myself and invent characters of my own.

The trouble was my Mr Micawbers and Uriah Heeps invariably turned out to be animals. Pigs, cows and bubbly-jocks. But at least I was getting the feel of words and the secret joy of seeing some of my inventions coming alive, if only in my own sight. And I have never forgotten that lame actor. Even now when I re-read Dickens I can still hear his sonorous voice. It seems as if he is reading the story with me.

The only chance we had as children to show our acting abilities came on April First. All Fools' Day, the day when by tradition we were allowed to let our imaginations run riot and tell lies to our hearts' content. The great thing was to keep a straight face and make the tarradiddles sound as convincing as possible. Hunting the gowk, we called it, a gowk having two meanings: a daftie and a cuckoo.

'Hunty gowk!' we cried in triumph when we caught someone napping, preferably a grown-up; but they, too, were at the game, and it was difficult not to be taken in by someone in authority when ordered, for example, to let the cat out of the milkhouse. 'She's got shut in, an' she'll lap up a' the cream, if ye dinna hurry.'

To go or not to go? Even Jessie was at it, with a face like a poker. 'Daursay, lassie, ye're no' takin' the measles? Ye've come oot in spots. Tak' a keek in the gless.' By the time I had reached the kitchen mirror, Jessie had cried, 'Hunty gowk!' and won the day.

Not so easy to fool her. I tried everything.

'Jessie! Jessie! You're wanted on the telephone. It's urgent,' I would cry, running after her as she was about to hang out the washing. It was a silly thing to say, for Jessie never answered the telephone, if she could help it. Thon noisy beast, she called it.

'Oh ay!' she would say disbelievingly. 'You answer it, lassie. If it's the king tell I'm ower thrang to speak to him.'

Try again. 'Oh look, Jessie! What's happened to that sheet? There's a great big hole in it. Look!'

But Jessie stubbornly refused to be drawn. With a clothes-peg in her mouth she muttered, 'Look yoursel'. Ye're no' catchin' me.'

If I let enough time elapse there was always the chance she might forget and I could catch her unawares, but it did not always work.

'Jessie! Jessie! The minister's on his way up the road. You're to come in and bake a scone. Hurry!'

'Tell the meenister to bake his ain scones.'

It was hopeless.

Jock-the-herd was a far easier target, but I sometimes thought he let himself be fooled just to please me.

'Jock, look out! Your pipe's burning a hole in your pocket.'

'Man-lassie, where aboot?'

'Hunty-gowk!'

My problem was how to tell when Jock was trying to gowk me.

'Man-lassie, rin for your life. The bull's got lowse an' he's in a terrible temper.'

It could be true. If so, there was no time to argue. The safest thing was to scramble over the dyke and never mind whether I was gowked or not.

Though it was all good fun April First was an uneasy kind of day, for if anything untoward did happen, who would believe it? For example, when the kitchen chimney went on fire. Jessie had been trying to clear away the soot by setting fire to pages of the *Scotsman* and thrusting them up the lum. I enjoyed watching this operation and always ran outside to see the sparks flying into the air. But today it was more than sparks. Smoke and flames came belching forth. I could hear a frenzied yell from Jessie. 'The lum's on haud. Rin an' fetch the men.'

I went tearing round to the work-stable to tell the hinds, but would they listen?

'I'm deif,' said Wull, continuing to curry-comb his Clydesdale's tail.

'Me, tae,' said Tam, who was sweeping out the stable. 'Awa' an' gowk somebody else.'

It was the herd and the Boss who finally had to come to the rescue. The hinds were horrified when they saw them up a ladder, scrambling on the roof, and rounded on me, 'Ye micht hae tell't us!'

If April First was a daft day April Second was equally full of nonsense. Paper-Tail Day, we called it in the Borders. A day when the local paper came into its own, for we made long paper trails of it and the *Scotsman*, and, armed with safety-pins, chose a victim to stalk in the hope of stealthily pinning a tail to the back of his jacket. Often blissfully unaware that we ourselves were trailing tails behind us.

This operation required great sleight of hand, for any fumbling gave the show away; and though it was comparatively easy to hoodwink our classmates, our greatest ambition was to tail Auld Baldy-Heid. We always held a council of war to decide who was to bell the cat. I can recall Big Bob slinking out of his seat and tiptoeing to the master who was writing on the blackboard, paper-tail and safety-pin at the ready. We held our breath while we watched him picking up Auld Baldy-Heid's jacket between finger and thumb. A gasp of relief when the deed was done and Big Bob was back in his seat, the hero of the hour.

It was difficult to stifle our mirth as Auld Baldy-Heid marched about the classroom with the long tail trailing behind him. Wee Maggie took a fit of the giggles and we all coughed and shuffled our feet, trying to cover it up.

'Less noise,' he reprimanded us sternly. 'Settle down and get on with your sums.'

It was when he settled down that the trouble started. In his haste Big Bob had not succeeded in fastening the safety-pin securely, with the result that Auld Baldy-Heid had no sooner sat down than he leapt to his feet, his face scarlet with rage.

'Who did it?' he roared, tearing off the offending safety-pin and the trailing tail. 'I'll murder the lot of you!'

But he knew and we knew he could not carry out his threat for it was an unwritten law that on Paper-Tail Day as on April First *we* were the ones who could get away with murder. But he got his revenge on April Third, which was an ordinary day.

Was any day ordinary?

Certainly not the one on which Jessie called out: 'There's a wee man in a kilt dancin' in the garden. Come an' see, lassie.'

If it had been Hunty Gowk day I would have known better than to look. But it wasn't, and there *was* a wee man in the garden dancing the Highland Fling amongst the flowers and nettles, with his tattered kilt swirling around his bare knees. He was diddling away to himself, making mouth-music, which came to a sudden stop when he ran out of breath. At which point he bowed to the kitchen window where we were watching, before scrambling over the candytuft to come in and get his reward.

He was a tramp, of course, but a performing one. A cut above the rest, he told us, as he accepted some coppers and a slice of bread and cheese. 'I gie value for siller. I'll do the sword dance, if ye like, wi' the poker an' tongs, ance I've got ma braith back.'

Yorky, too – one of our regulars – sometimes entertained us by waving his arms wildly and giving us a long screed. Shakespeare, he said, but it sounded more like mumbo-jumbo to us.

Then came the wonderful day when I was taken by my parents all the way to Edinburgh to see real drama in a real theatre. We were to go to something called a matinée. The word itself was fascinating enough, let alone the journey to Auld Reekie, beginning as it did with a dawn drive to Jedburgh to catch the local train, then changing along the line to the express which whirled us to Waverley.

The theatre! Never had I seen anything like it, even in my imagination. The plush seats, the rich red curtains hiding the stage, the whirls and whorls on the ceiling, the exciting sounds of the orchestra tuning up, and the audience. I wondered if the people in the boxes were lords and ladies. Even the programme sellers seemed to be part of the play, and I would not have cared if the curtain never rose, there was so much to see all around me.

But it did go up after the orchestra had played a haunting overture, and from then on I was in a trance. It was better even than listening to the lame actor at Southdean. Here were real characters living out their private lives before our very eyes, involving us all in their joys and sorrows. Sometimes I felt like an eavesdropper and turned my head away at the love-scenes. I thought we ought not to be looking and listening. There was no privacy on the stage.

The heroine, poor pathetic creature, was in a state of agitation from start to finish. I longed to comfort her as she sank to her knees, sobbing bitterly and calling upon God to help her. She carried a baby in her arms, dressed in long clothes, hiding it against her breast so that we could not see its face. I wondered if it was a real baby or only a wax doll like the Holy Child in the procession.

I cannot recollect the plot, only that the heroine had walked all the way from Scotland to London still carrying the bairn in her arms to plead with the queen for a re-prieve for her sister. (Later on, I learned that the play was about Jeannie Deans and her sister Effie, from Sir Walter Scott's *Heart of Midlothian*). There was a heart-rending scene with the heroine kneeling before the throne – or was it only a chair? – where the queen sat in full regalia.

Was the reprieve granted? I hope so. All I can remember is the actress's wild hair, her ragged skirt, her bare feet and her cries of supplication as she clutched the far-travelled baby to her bosom.

There was an interval halfway through when the lights suddenly went up and we were jerked from one world to another. It was almost like being reborn. The usherettes brought round little trays with cups of tea and biscuits while the orchestra played some waltz tunes heard above the tinkle of teaspoons. All very well for us, but what about the poor heroine still stumbling along the hard road to London?

It was surprising to see how the cast suddenly sloughed off their stage-characters and became themselves when they took their curtain calls at the end. Even the dead walked, while friends and foes alike joined hands and came forward to bow. Jeannie and Effie Deans, all smiles now, and minus the baby, dropped graceful curtsies in their ragged gowns, holding hands on equal terms with the queen herself.

It was all very puzzling. Fantasy and reality merging into one. It was not till I got home and heard Jessie saying, 'Dinna mak' a slaister on the kitchen flair,' that I got a grip on myself.

She, at least, was real enough.

10. Playing a Part

But were we not all playing a part most of the time? Putting it on.

Most people's lives, I suspected, were made up of a mixtures of reality and pretence. Even Liz-Ann, the Cairthorse, had a private paradise of her own, far removed from the humdrum routine of rubbing and scrubbing. Sometimes I saw a secret smile lighting up her plain face as she polished the kitchen cutlery with emery paper.

'What are you thinking about, Liz-Ann?' I once asked her.

The Cairthorse gave a guilty start and dropped a fork on the floor. Her face went scarlet as if her most personal secrets had been revealed. 'I'm no' lettin' on,' she said and turned her head away to hide her thoughts from my prying eyes.

I felt ashamed that I had tried to probe. Our thoughts were amongst the few precious private things we possessed. Luckily, no one could tune into them like the wireless.

Ours – the wireless – frequently broke down. The aerial, trailing over a high tree, was battered by winds, or became entangled with bullocks' horns, so that all we could hear were strange sounds called atmospherics. But when it was working at full strength Father liked to share its highlights with the folk on the farm.

'That's the Savoy Orpheans' Dance Band,' he would tell them, turning it up to its loudest pitch. 'All the way from London.'

The hinds shook their heads in disbelief. It was a bit too much to swallow. A dance band playing in London and being heard at Overton Bush.

'Haggis-bags!' said the herd (which was his strongest word for 'rubbish!'). 'Thon's a terrible dirdum.' He had managed all these years without the Savoy Orpheans and saw no reason to enthuse about them now.

The men were all invited in on Armistice Day to 'hear the silence', standing in an uneasy group with their bunnets under their arms. The silence seemed to last for hours and I never knew where to look when the Last Post was sounded. The men stared at the floor, and I tried to think of the soldiers who never came marching home. Black Sandy, who drove the school bus, had been at Wypers and sometimes sang about 'Mademoiselle from Armentiers'. His French accent should have been better than mine since he had actually lived with the Froggies, but it was terrible. Miss Crichton would have killed him.

It was easy to see that Father played many roles, apart from being Boss on the farm. That, I think, was the one he liked least. Often he had to pull himself together to remember his responsibilities and would sooner have been singing 'O Dem Golden Slippers' in the Darkey Troupe.

They still talk about it today in the Borders, Father and his Darkey Troupe. There were others involved of course, but he was the guiding spirit. Auld Baldy-Heid, his face as black as soot, plonking away at a banjo. The gardener from the Big Hoose dressed in the laird's pyjamas (most working-men did not possess such garments, preferring nightsarks instead) trying to talk in a Sambo accent while telling his terrible jokes.

'Say, Boss, what am de best way to make de Swiss roll?'

'I dunno, Sambo,' Father would say solemnly, staring at him with soot-rimmed eyes. 'What am de best way to make de Swiss roll?'

'Push him down de mountainside. He-he-he!'

The audience loved it and Father was in his element. Sometimes the hinds would chap at the kitchen door and ask where he was.

'Up in the greenhoose,' Jessie would tell them.

I would be sent to the top garden to fetch him. Maybe he would be sorting out seedlings or just sitting in a wheelbarrow amongst a clutter of plant pots, playing the jew's harp, reading the Squeaker, or just away in a world of his own.

'What aboot the Lang Field, then?' Tam or Wull would ask him once I had brought him back to life. There was no sir-ing given or expected.

'The Lang Field?' Oh ay, I'll take a look at it.'

Sometimes I saw him writing things on his cuffs. A new joke for Sambo, maybe, or a reminder about the Lang Field?

Occasionally on market days he called for me at the Grammar School gates and drove me home in the motor. I felt quite proud to be going in it instead of the bus, but there was no guarantee I would get home any quicker. Often the bus shot past us when we were stuck on a brae, with Tin Lizzie rolling back and Father shouting, 'Whoa!' as he struggled with the gears.

Mother, like everyone else, had a private and a public face. Sometimes she looked at herself in the small keekingglass on the kitchen wall, and suddenly the harassed housewife was transformed into a young girl. Fair-haired round-cheeked, rosy-lipped, and with a sparkle in her eyes. She would pull herself up, smile at her image as if flirting with herself. 'Mirror, mirror, on the wall.' Then the clumsy Cairthorse would drop a dish on the floor, and the image, like the plate, was shattered.

I think Mother saw herself as a lady. Certainly she looked like one when dressed up in her fur coat. She always wore good shoes and gloves. And attractive hats which Father bought in a big shop in Edinburgh. I often wondered if he tried them on himself. They always suited her, and had a bit of style about them.

I can see her swathed in a motoring veil, sitting beside Father as they set off on a private jaunt on their own, This is what they liked best, to go off unencumbered by any small fry. On such occasions I felt rejected and in need of compensation. Something sweet to eat. I craved for toffee and would coax Jessie to make a boiling, or, breaking all rules, would make it myself which usually ended with the pan being burnt and the toffee uneatable.

When darkness fell I went and peered out of the dining-room window looking for the car-lights. I would stay there for ages sucking burnt toffee and seeing visions in the starry sky. When the lights at last appeared I felt a great sense of relief and shouted, 'They're coming!' Then I would settle down to my book as if I was indifferent to their comings and goings. Let them see how little I cared where they had been or how late they returned!

We were all shut away inside ourselves like crabs. What lay under Jessie's hard exterior? There must have been something there for she read Annie S. Swan's stories and gave a sigh of satisfaction when they ended happily.

'That's Alison Macrae settled doon wi' John Lindsay at last. Ay, it's a guid match, that.' She nodded her approval as she laid the *People's Friend* aside, and for a time there was a faraway look in her eyes. Was she perhaps seeing herself as Alison settling down with John to a life of married bliss? No use asking her; I would only get a skelp on the lug.

What a pity none of us ever really knew each other.

The only person who gave way to his feelings and revealed every thought that came into his daft head was Yorky the tramp. He did not care who was listening. Anybody or nobody. He wandered the countryside, swiping at imaginary enemies with his walking-stick and roaring out his ramblings to hedges, ditches, cats, dogs and people alike.

'You!' he would shout to me if we met face to face. 'A piece of rubbish. You're all rubbish, nothing but rubbish. I,' he would go on, pulling himself upright, 'I am the king of the roads. What do *you* know about anything? Nothing! Now, I'll tell you what *I* think . . .'

And he would, with so much mixed-up rhetoric that I was none the wiser at the end than the beginning, but it seemed to do Yorky good to get it off his chest. After a spout of speech he would calm down and a saner look come into his wild eyes. 'I want tea, bread and cheese and a place to sleep. You'll see to it.' He was like an overlord instructing one of his varlets. No begging or mooching. Yorky demanded attention. It was his right as king of the roads. He had played the part for so long that it was second nature to him.

What part did I play?

It varied from day to day. Mostly I saw myself through rose-coloured spectacles, a ministering angel beloved by everyone, so helpful that the world could never have got on without me. I could hear people singing my praises. 'Her! She's perfect. Never thinks of herself, always of other folk. Worth her weight in gold.' I basked in their adulation, every word deserved.

It was as well Jessie was there to push me off my high horse. 'Here, you!' slapping a wet dishcloth into my hand. 'Stop smirkin' to yoursel' an' wesh the dishes. Ye're nae ornament so ye micht as weel be usefu'.' Certainly Jessie's spectacles were made of plain glass.

I made a conscious effort to be a different person at the Grammar School, curbing my country ways and striving to keep in line with the others. I felt quite sophisticated as I strolled up the High Street at lunchtime. A townee, accustomed to traffic, more or less neatly dressed, recognised by the shopkeepers. What if they saw the real me running wild on the farm, swinging on gates, climbing trees, riding workhorses and stooking corn? Try as I did to get rid of them, there were still many rough edges.

Several times I had been invited to visit classmates' homes. Their lives were so different from mine that I would have been ashamed to return the invitations. Town households ran on smoother lines. No hitty-missy meals, no clattering sounds from the kitchen, no shouts from Jock-the-herd: 'Man-lassie, come oot an' help to weir in the soo.' No Cairthorses dropping dishes on the floor.

All the same I did not enjoy my visits. The houses were too overheated, the windows too closely shut, the rooms cluttered with furnishings. At the tea-table I could never do justice to the lavish meals, nor could I just sit still and watch, for the conversation was directed at me as the visitor. I racked my brains for something bright to say.

'The cow's going to calve.'

'Oh yes, dear?' A blank look from my hostess. 'Have another piece of pie. No? What a poor appetite you have for a country lass.'

A country lass. That was how they saw me, in spite of all my efforts to play a more polished part. What would they think if they saw the real me at home?

The day inevitably came.

It was forced upon me by none other than Lucy, the ewe-lamb, who had long been hinting that she would love to visit the farm and was consumed with curiosity to see how I lived 'out in the wilds'. She visualised it, I felt sure, as a kind of zoo with myself as one of the inmates, shut up in a cage or a pigsty.

'My dad's got a new car and we always go for a run on Saturday. We could easily come.'

I ignored all her hints. Then they became demands. 'You'll *have* to ask us. I want to come.' Lucy usually got what she wanted in the end.

One day she told me triumphantly, 'It's all arranged! We're coming on Saturday. Me and my mum and dad in the new car.'

And that was it.

There was no putting her off. I would sooner it had been Jeannie, another of my classmates, who was nicer in every way, but her father did not own a car, old or new.

'They'll just have to take us as they find us,' Mother said when I broke the news to her. She went the length of baking dropscones and a sponge-cake, but there was no setting out of the best china or the lace-edged tablecloth. It was the Cairthorse's afternoon off, and Jessie was working in the fields. So we would be left to serve ourselves with as little ceremony as possible. What would the ewe-lamb, accustomed to a maid with cap and apron, think of our common ways?

I was the only worried one. The others pursued their normal ways, Father digging in the garden in his shirt-sleeves, Mother gathering the eggs from the henhouses with a basket over her arm, and not even changed into her best blouse.

I ran about the house trying to tidy it up, straightening cushions, picking the baby's bricks from the floor, dusting the sideboard, putting a vase of flowers on the table. I wished the visitors could have seen it properly set with a snowy-white cloth and the silver epergne in the centre.

All of a sudden I felt ashamed of myself, realising I was in danger of becoming a snob. On an impulse I tore off my shoes and stockings in disgust and went about barefoot as I always did on Saturdays. Let them think what they liked. Who cared? I had a good mind to go and sit beside Grumphy in the pigsty. Instead, I found myself keeping a watchful eye on the road to see if the car was coming.

At last.

'That's them!' I cried, scurrying out in my bare feet.

'Ay!' said father, calmly laying down his spade as the car purred into sight, scattering cocks and hens out of its path. 'Hullo,' he called to the visitors, rolling down his sleeves and going forward to meet them.

'What a road!' groaned Lucy's father in an aggrieved voice, leaning out of the driving-seat to examine the mud on his car wheels. 'You should get something done about it.'

'So I should,' agreed Father evenly. 'I hope the car's none the worse. Come away in.'

They trooped out of the car and I was horrified to see Father leading them in by the kitchen door. 'It's nearer!' I felt my face flush as I saw them stare at the stone floor, the hams hanging from the ceiling, the meal-bins, the sheep-dip calendar on the wall, then at my bare feet.

The ewe-lamb was dressed to kill in a blue velvet frock, a straw hat with ribbons floating down the back, white socks and patent leather shoes. Quite the lady. Jessie would have designated her a wee madam.

'Through here,' called Mother from the dining-room. She had come in from her egg-gathering and was at the table buttering the dropscones. 'You'll be ready for a cup of tea.'

The ewe-lamb did not like dropscones. Nor raspberry jam which was in the middle of the sponge-cake. 'Run and fetch the gooseberry,' Mother told me.

'Don't like gooseberry.'

'Well, what about strawberry? I think there's a pot left in the jam cupboard.'

I went to fetch it and the ewe-lamb graciously accepted a thin piece of bread and butter liberally spread with strawberry jam. Then she partook of a chocolate biscuit, a packet of which mother had produced out of the blue. One, then another, and a third.

'She likes the taste of chocolate,' said her mother, fondly watching every bite. 'It'll do her good. She's a bit delicate, you know.'

'I'm finished,' said Lucy, licking the chocolate from her fingers and shuffling restlessly in her seat.

'Show her round,' said Mother, dismissing me from the table, though I had not sampled the sponge-cake, far less reached the chocolate biscuit stage.

The ewe-lamb followed me around the house, upstairs as well as down. 'What's that?' she asked when we came to the garret door.

'The gaol. I get shut up there sometimes.'

'What for?'

'Being bad.' Though more often I was shut in for doing good deeds that misfired.

Lucy gave me a smug look and said, 'I'm never bad.' I could see her halo shining round her head.

In the parlour she went and thumped on the piano. She could play louder than I did, but no better. Then, having poked into cupboards and presses, pulled out drawers, fingered ornaments, tugged at the bell-rope which jangled unanswered in the kitchen, she asked, 'Is that all?'

'Well, there's outside. Come and see the calves.'

She hung back.

'Will they bite?'

'No, of course not.'

But outside was not a success. She let out a scream the moment the bubblyjock came running to us on his splay feet, and turned up her nose at the smell in the byre. When a calf tried to nibble at her fingers she hit out at it angrily.

'Keep away, you nasty thing!'

There was nothing she liked. The corn-barn with rats rustling in the corner, the henhouse where a clocker was sitting on her clutch of eggs and pecked out at us when disturbed, the pigsty where Grumphy and the piglets were routing about in the swill. Even the prospect of climbing a haystack did not appeal to her. 'Oh no! Not in my good clothes.'

So in the end I gave up and left her to pick her own way through the puddles while I went and sat on the swing. I could see Father showing her parents his sweet-peas in the top garden. He gathered a big bunch for them to take home, and Mother gave them some fresh eggs and butter.

'Come again,' said Mother as they got into the car, but I could hear the false note in her voice. I waved from the swing. The wave, too, was false.

'It must be dreadfully dull for you away out here,' I heard Lucy's mother say.

'We manage,' said Father, closing the door on her.

'You'll remember to get something done about that road,' the ewe-lamb's father said as they were moving off.

'I'll remember,' Father said with no conviction in his voice. 'Safe home!'

When they had gone I wanted to rush forward and thank my parents for putting up with them. I felt proud of Father and Mother for playing their parts so well; but as usual the words stuck in my throat and I could not express my feelings. I realised, though, how lucky I was. *They* were made of the right stuff.

As Father rolled up his sleeves and went back to his gardening and Mother set about clearing the tea-table, I felt increasingly thankful that *I* was not a pampered only child.

11. Change and Decay

I cannot recall being bored as a child; it was not a word in common use in the Borders. But there were times when I desired something different to happen, just to alter the pattern of life a little. Then when it did, it was not what I wanted at all. Go back! Let everything be the same as before!

It even disturbed me at the spring-cleaning when Mother and Jessie shifted the chairs or the piano to different places in the parlour, or when they changed the curtains. I liked the faded ones best. They were old friends, and though they would not be discarded altogether, for doubtless they would be cut up and transformed into a summer frock for me, as well as cushion-covers for the sofa, it took me ages to become accustomed to the new ones.

One of the sad dirges we sang at the kirk warned us about change and decay in all around we see; but I for one kept my eyes firmly shut. All the same, I would be forced to open them soon, for whether I liked it or not, big changes were on the way.

I think I first became aware of them when it was announced that we were to go on holiday that summer to Swinside Townhead.

'Where?' I asked incredulously. For once I did not believe a word Jessie said.

'Soonside Toonheid,' she said, translating it into local language in case I had not comprehended.

'But why on earth . . . ?'

Why on earth go on holiday to that other farm away in the Oxnam district at the back of beyond, which father rented from the great Duke of Roxburghe? The farmhouse was falling to pieces and the grieve and his wife who lived in it were a fushionless pair. The ground was sour and nothing seemed to flourish on the farm. Even the cocks and hens looked peelly-wally.

Father went there once a week or so to keep an eye on things and always came back with furrows on his brow. It was always the same story. Some piece of machinery had broken down, the lackadaisical grieve had forgotten to do this or that. The whining wife with her brood of ailing children did nothing to make things better. Indeed, doing nothing was what they were both best at.

So what kind of holiday was it going to be?

I would sooner have stayed in my castle on the hill or lived up a tree like a squirrel.

It had never mattered at the village school if I could not put up my hand when Auld Baldy-Heid said, 'Hands up those who are going away on holiday.' Most of my classmates just stayed at home and ran wild. The holiday was being away from Auld Baldy-Heid.

But it was different at the Grammar School. Every hand shot up, everyone was going somewhere. One lad, a fellow-sufferer in the Latin class, was going to London to stay with his godmother. (I could not picture what kind of relative *that* was.) Others were going to the sea-side; but the ewe-lamb beat the lot of us by announcing she was being taken abroad by her doting parents. Not just over the Carter Bar into England but to the real Abroad away in a foreign land. We would never hear the end of it.

'Brussels!' she said, looking more than ever like a cat who has licked up all the cream. It was a wonder *she* had no godmother, but it was her father's cousin who lived there. 'Mum and Dad say it will be good for my French. Wait till I come back. Mary-Ann Crichton won't half get a surprise.'

I wondered where she was going. Mary-Ann. Back to her home in Aberdeen, maybe. And the other teachers. What about the science master? If he had been coming with us to the back of beyond the holiday might have been worthwhile.

I avoided the subject but when I was directly faced with it, said defiantly, 'I'm going to Swinside Townhead.'

'Is it in England?' I was asked.

'No, it's in Oxnam.'

'Goodness! you're not going very far,' said Lucy, tossing her ringlets.

Too far for me. 'Could I not just stay at home?' I asked Jessie.

'No! Ye're a' gaun. The hale clamjamfry.' No escape.

It was difficult to fathom the complicated minds of grown-ups, but I gathered it had something to do with Mother being pregnant, though Jessie would never put *that* into words, and something to do with Father deciding at last to take a closer look at what the grieve was doing, or not doing.

So, with little enthusiasm, I gathered together a few possessions and bundled myself along with the rest into the motor. My elder brother and sister, home from their colleges, were to cycle over on their own. Lucky things!

they had real bicycles with proper wheels, tyres, spokes and everything.

'Ta-ta,' I said dismally to Jessie, hovering at the kitchen door. 'I wish we were on our way back.'

'Guid riddance!' she said predictably and waved her apron, but I think at heart she felt sorry for me.

It was worse, much worse, than I had feared. Misery from start to finish. For one thing it rained relentlessly every day, adding to the discomfort of the draughty farmhouse and turning the yard into a quagmire of mud and puddles. The drookit fowls stood about pecking aimlessly in the glaur and hunching their backs, trying to find comfort under their wet feathers.

There was none for me.

Though the droopy grieve and his missis had made an effort to clean the place up – there was an old besom still lying on the sagging sofa beside a pile of unwashed garments which had been hastily tidied into a heap – the whole house smelt foosty, the cracked cups had rims of dirt round the edges, the milk was turned, the fire smoked, and many of the window panes were cracked.

'We meant to get them mended,' apologised the missis, hitching up her torn skirt and fastening it at the waist with a safety-pin, 'but himself has never had time to get round to it. He's been bad with his chest, and then the binder broke down.' On and on, always apologising.

The smoky fire gave out little heat. The sticks were wet. 'Himself forgot to take them under cover. He had to see to the sow when it got lost, and we've run out of coal. We meant to order more, but you know how it is. There's always so much to do.'

And so little done. Jessie would have had a fit if she had seen the ashes still in the grate, rust and dirt everywhere.

When it came to allocating sleeping-quarters there was no place left for me except a bumpy mattress laid on the floor of 'the room' where the windows were stuck and had not been opened for years. But that was the least of it. It was the lost feeling of being in limbo away from anything familiar or any kindred spirit that brought me almost to the depths of despair. I did not know where to turn for comfort.

It was certainly not a bookish household, except for the bible used to prop up the kitchen table. In any case, where could I have sat down quietly to read? The snivelling children swarmed after me like puppies, and the peevish baby, known as the runt (the last of a litter), was teething and let everyone know it. He was a wizened little creature, more like an old man than a baby. I wondered if he could be a changeling and if the Little Folk had stolen the real baby away and left the runt in his place. All the children, poor things, were unattractive, skinny and spotty-faced, dressed in garments handed down one to the other and seldom put in the wash-tub.

Still, it was one of them, the most unattractive, with missing teeth and a 'gleg e'e', like her father's, who helped unknowingly to set me on my road to story-telling.

Elsie always referred to herself in the third person. 'Elthie wanth a thtory,' she would lisp, dumping herself down on the dirty floor at my feet. 'Tell Elthie a thtory.'

She was a little pest but I sympathised with her in a way, knowing my own thirst for stories. It was hard going, for no sooner had I finished one than Elsie would say, 'Elthie wanth another thtory. Tell Elthie . . . '

The rest of the brood, for want of anything better to do, gathered round, too, and sometimes even the runt stopped crying.

The stories were variations of Jessie's milking-time tales, all about beasts. Others I dredged up from somewhere in my head, about tattie-bogles, bubblyjocks and real adventures like the time I got lost in the snow.

Elthie liked that best.

'Again! Elthie wanth the thtory about the thnow.'

I had to tell and re-tell the stories so often that I suddenly decided I might as well write them down. So, with a blunt pencil and pages torn from one of the children's jotters, I started off to become an Author, helped and hindered by Elsie.

'Thtop writing. Elthie wanth a thtory.'

After several disastrous meals Mother took over the cooking and I helped by setting tables and washing dishes, while the missis drooped around in her down-at-heel slippers, shoogling the peevish runt in her arms, with a dummy in his mouth to stem his whines. Now and again she said to herself, 'I must get on,' but she never did.

My elder brother and sister escaped after a couple of days. They just got on to their bikes and cycled home. I would willingly have walked it, over hill and dale, but when I broached the subject Mother said, 'You bide where you are and make yourself useful. You can peel the potatoes.'

One day when there was a faint glimmer of light shining through the rain clouds I put on an old torn waterproof which I found hanging in the lobby. Feeling that I must escape I ran out through the muddy yard up past the cottages and away to the Back of Beyond where there was nothing to see but the Cheviots, a different view from the one at home, but they were the same hills.

I had the vague intention of going on and on and vanishing into the distance, I was so fed up with everything and everybody. Who would miss me, anyway? Jessie maybe and Jock-the-herd. 'Maybe ay and maybe hooch-ay!'

Yet would it not be a pity to end my life before I had fulfilled myself in any way? If God knew every blade of grass and had bothered to count the hairs on my head, surely He must have some purpose for me here on earth. But what?

I was soon to find out.

At first I could not believe my ears when I heard the

sound of moaning, or my eyes when I saw the man lying by the roadside with blood oozing from a deep gash on his brow and his leg doubled up beneath him. His bicycle lay beside him, its wheels buckled and the handlebar twisted. It looked a worse wreck than my old boneshaker at home.

'Are you hurt?' I asked him. A silly question, with blood trickling down his face and him groaning with pain.

'It's ma leg. Canna move it. Fell aff ma bike.'

Small wonder, too, on such a rutted road.

My heart was bumping and I began to panic, wondering what was the best thing to do in such a crisis. At the same time I realised that here at last was a situation where I must show my mettle. 'Use your rummlegumption, lassie.'

The best thing, I decided, would be to run back to the farm as quickly as possible and get the men to come and help. But first I fumbled up my sleeve where I knew I had tucked a hankie. Clean for once, but soon saturated in blood when I took it out and pressed it to the man's brow. He kept hold of it, trying to stem the flow. His face was ashen and I wondered it he was about to faint, or even die.

'Wait here,' I told him. As if he could have moved! 'I'll away and get the men to help. We won't be long.'

'Thanks, lass,' he said faintly.

I sprinted back towards Swinside Townhead faster than I had ever run before, even at the Sports, splashing through puddles, never mind my pounding heart or the stitch in my side. At last I was doing *something*. It seemed miles longer than when I came along the road only a short while ago. I had no purpose in life then. Now I felt like the saviour of all mankind, of one man, anyway. The rain was pouring again. He would get his death of cold if he had to lie helpless there by the wayside for long. Run faster!

At last the cottages came in sight. The first person I saw was the grieve with an old sack over his droopy shoulders, leaning on the garden gate in conversation with Tamson, the Swinside shepherd.

Tamson was not a patch on Jock-the-herd but better than nobody in an emergency and the grieve at any time. So it was to him that I blurted out my story in great gulps of words, not bothering to make them into sentences. But he got the gist of it and said, sensibly enough. 'Ye'd better see the Boss. He's got the motor. Tell him I'll come wi' him.'

'Where is he?' I asked urgently.

'Doon at the fermhoose.'

I raced the few hundred yards down to the house and there was Father with the motor at the gate, tinkering with Tin Lizzie's internals.

Once more I told my garbled story. Father, with a dirty rag in his hand, looked at me doubtfully.

'You're not making it up? It's not one of your stories?'

'No, it's not!' I cried, deeply hurt.

Was this all he thought of me? What a reputation! A teller of tarradiddles. But this was no time to take offence.

'It's true!' I insisted, fiercely. 'We'll need to hurry or the man'll bleed to death. Tamson's coming to help. He's waiting up the road.

At last Father seemed to be convinced. He slammed down the bonnet of the car. 'Right! Hop in, lass, and I'll see if she'll start. The rain's got into her.'

The motor was difficult to crank up at the best of times. I waited impatiently while Father turned the starting-handle, listening for the welcome sound of the engine puttering into life. Try, try, try again.

At last. Tin Lizzie took the tremors and began to shudder and shake. Father got into the driving-seat and we set off up the road to find the grieve still leaning on the gate and Tamson ready to shuffle into the back seat. He had brought a length of rope with him, though what he meant to do with it I could only surmise; tie the battered bicycle on to the back of the car, maybe. But it was the thought of the maimed man that was worrying me.

Hurry! Hurry! I prayed that the engine would not stall as we pressed on through the lashing rain past the cottages to the Back of Beyond.

'Just round the next corner,' I cried, shoogling to and fro as if that would make the motor go faster. The windscreen wipers were stuck as usual and it was difficult to see out. But what was there to see?

Nothing!

When we reached the spot where the man had been lying there was no trace of him, not even the wreck of his bicycle.

Could I have made a mistake? Was it round the next corner?

'No, it was here,' I insisted to myself and to Father who was banging on the brakes.

One thing was clear. He was not here now. Not a sign of him. Tamson scrambled out, clutching the rope and glowering at me as if he was about to twist it round my neck and hang me from the nearest tree; but it was Father's look and his words to the shepherd that hurt me most.

'Sorry about this, Tamson. She's a daft, lassie, always imagining things. Her head's full of nonsense.'

My lip began to tremble. 'It's not nonsense,' I protested, and then realised it was no use. I was completely discredited with no means of defending myself. Completely bamboozled, too, for how could the man have vanished and him so badly hurt? I *knew* he had been there, but how could I convince them?

I could see by the black looks on the men's faces that anything I said would only fan their anger into flames. And now I began to have doubts myself. Was I really a story-teller, making it all up? No, I was not! I felt for my hankie up my sleeve. It was not there. It was no proof, of course, but it gave me a modicum of assurance. I searched the roadside for any sign of blood, but the rain must have washed it away.

To add to the general misery the motor refused to re-start. Tamson and father had to push her to the side of the road. 'She's maybe needing petrol,' Father said. He never forgot to give Flora her nosebag but sometimes overlooked the fact that Tin Lizzie, too, required regular sustenance. 'I think I left some in a tin in the shed.'

'I'll go back and get it,' I volunteered, hoping to regain a measure of respect. Father did not indicate his approval or otherwise of my offer, so I walked back in the pouring rain like a bedraggled sparrow. The fact that I was soaked through to the skin did not bother me. I was too busy puzzling over the affair and smarting at Father's dismissal of me as a daft lassie.

How did he know what kind of a person I was? I could have analysed him, in a sort of a way, for I had watched and studied him closely. And did *he* not elaborate some-times his dreams and his stories. But the unfair thing was that *I* had not elaborated. I had told the plain truth, though there was nobody to know that, except God if He had been watching.

As I was plodding towards the cottages I heard a familiar rattling sound behind me. Tin Lizzie chugging along like a steam roller. Father did not stop to pick me up. He did not even toot or wave, but swept by splashing up a great stream of water which caught me fair and square in the face. I was so wet already I hardly noticed it, and to do him justice he may have realised that, once he had got it started, it would have been imprudent of him to stop the tempera-mental motor again, and I was near enough my destination, anyway. At least I would not have to trudge back with the tin of petrol.

When I entered the untidy kitchen the grieve's children

were crawling about on the floor playing with a scabby kitten.

'Elthie wanth a thtory,' she said, clutching at my wet legs.

But I said 'No' in a firm voice, determined to live down my reputation. 'No more stories!'

12. Revelations

It was a few days later that Mother said to me, 'Dress yourself properly. We're going out to tea.' She did not say where.

Dressing properly meant putting on shoes and stockings, my one good frock, brushing and replaiting my tousled hair, seeing that my face and hands were clean, and getting myself into the right mood for company. Mother looked the part when she put on her costume and a little toque hat with a veil. Father changed into his dark suit, and we were off.

I sat in the back of the motor wondering in which direction we would go. Up past the cottages to the Back of Beyond. I averted my gaze when we came to the spot where I had left the man lying by the roadside. I was still confused at the outcome of that dark episode. It rankled so much that I tried to put it out of my mind.

In any case, I was soon kept fully occupied, getting out to open the creaky gates barring our way across the side-road. Getting in and out of the motor was easier than jumping in and out of the gig, but opening the gates always presented a problem, for some were fastened with complicated cleeks and others tied with bindertwine. It was a heinous sin to leave them open, so I had to wait till Tin Lizzie was driven through and refasten them before taking my place in the motor again. I was being useful, if nothing else, though the operation did my clean stockings no good. The ground was still squelchy, and muddy water splattered up on me from the motor's wheels.

We were aiming, I could see, for a remote farmhouse hidden amongst trees in the foothills of the Cheviots where a friend of Father's lived with his prim sisters. Nothing prim about their brother. He had the reputation of being the wild man of the Borders, especially when he had the drink taken. No opening or shutting of gates for him when he was rollicking home late at night after one of his sprees. Singing at the pitch of his voice he drove his battle-stained car at them like a battering-ram and went straight through, leaving one of his men to come and repair the damage next morning.

His exploits, vastly exaggerated, were the speak of the countryside and could have filled pages of the Squeaker each week. Everybody liked him, no matter how much they tut-tutted. His swashbuckling attitude to life gave a bit of colour to the Oxnam district.

He seemed sober and upright enough today as he came forward to greet us and help Mother out of the car. But it was not him I looked at. It was another man, one of our host's farm-hands, who came limping forward. A man with a bruise on his forehead. The man I had left lying by the roadside.

'It's *him*!' I burst out, feeling a great load falling off my shoulders, now that I could prove – if only to myself – that I was not just a daft lassie making up silly stories.

'Hullo, lass.' The man came nearer, put his hand in his

pocket and brought out my handkerchief, the bloodstains removed. 'This is yours. Mr Will, the master, came by in his car and picked me up; but thanks for your help.'

'Daft deevil!' said Mr Will, the master (as if *he* had never strayed from the paths of righteousness himself). 'His bike'll never be the same again, and he's as lame as an old horse.'

'See!' I said triumphantly to Father, showing him my hankie in case he had not understood the whole import of the tale; but if I was waiting for him to say 'Sorry!' I waited in vain.

Neither he nor Mother made any comment. I could understand them, I suppose, for company manners had taken over, and the ladies of the house had come to the door to welcome their visitors. Family affairs must take a back seat. Perhaps they would mention it later on, on the way home, but I thought it unlikely. The subject was closed, so I just crept back into my shell and shook hands with the Misses Something who each made the predictable comment, 'My! isn't she shooting up?' before ushering us into the house.

They were a 'bein' family; that is, comfortably-off, and the house showed it. Everything was good, though old-fashioned, and the ladies kept up some sort of style even though they lived so far away in the wilderness.

We sat in the drawing-room (all plush cushions, footstools, antimacassars and brocade curtains) except brother William who roamed around like a stray dog not knowing where to settle. When he came near me he tugged my pigtails for something to do, and now and again his sisters would say, 'Sit down, William, and take your ease,' but *they* had had more practice, I could see, at sitting still and making polite conversation.

In their young days they had been sent to a Ladies' Seminary where they had learned good manners and never forgotten them. Not so Mr Will, who did not care a button for social frills.

Sometimes he said an aside to Father about farm affairs, but it was the sisters who kept the conversational ball rolling, tossing it back and forth to each other as if playing ping-pong, with an occasional side-throw to Mother. The weather kept them going for ages. Hadn't it been dreadful? All that rain! They had been thinking of taking a trip to Edinburgh and maybe staying there for a fortnight with some cousins. I saw a 'Good riddance!' look on brother William's face, but he restrained himself from picking up the dropped ball.

When the tea came in with all the paraphernalia of sugar-tongs, slop-basin, and wee lace-edged table-napkins, he refused the delicate china cup that was handed to him. 'Tea! Can't stand the stuff!' But he did his best in his clumsy fashion to hand round the plates of food. When he passed me the seed-cake I wished I had the courage to say, 'Seed-cake! Can't stand the stuff!' but I meekly accepted it and tried to get rid of the seeds as surreptitiously as I could.

The family photograph album was lying conpicuously on a nearby table. Were we going to have to suffer *that* after tea? It was more than brother William could bear.

'Come on, John,' he said, tugging at Father's arm. 'Ben to the parlour,' where, no doubt, he kept a stronger tipple than tea.

Father did his best not to seem too eager, but went off with a look of relief on his face after excusing himself to his hostesses. How I wished I could follow suit!

Now that the men were away the ladies' tongues were loosened and they began to talk more freely to Mother. Mostly about brother William and his exploits, though I doubt if they knew the half.

'He's such a good lad, William, but a little wild, you know. Sometimes he gets carried away . . . '

Mother nodded understandingly while I watched the
ladies leaning towards her as their talk became more
confidential. Like hens confabbing together, clucking
about the absent cockerel. After a time I did not strain
my ears to listen, though the word 'baby' seemed to have
entered into the conversation. The sisters were whispering
something about Mother's pregnancy, too delicate for my
ears to hear.

The eldest gave a warning glance at her sister and said
to me, 'Would you like to go through to the kitchen,
dear, and see Aggie?'

'Oh yes, please!'

I was on my feet, almost tripping over a sheepskin
rug in my haste to get away. Along a dark passage past
the parlour door from behind which I could hear the
cheerful sounds of talk, laughter, and glasses clinking.
Father and Mr Will were getting on a treat.

Aggie's kitchen was cosier than ours at home. There
was a carpet on the floor, easy-chairs to sit in, and pot-
plants on the window-sill. Aggie, as plump as a partridge,
was sitting with her feet on the fender, with a cup of tea
beside her and her skirt turned back to keep it from being
scorched. She was in her good black afternoon uniform
with a white cap on her head, but had taken off her starched
apron while she sat at ease.

'Are they needin' mair scones, or wantin' the teapot
filled?'

'No, they're not wanting anything, Aggie. I just came
to see you.'

I sat down on the rug beside her, not caring whether
I was scorched or not. This was my proper place. I could
equate with Aggie better than with her perjinct mis-
tresses.

'My! ye're fairly shootin' up. Hoo are ye keepin'?'

'I'm fine. How are you, Aggie?'

'Oh, I'm jacko!' (Jacko, I assumed, meant she was in

good fettle.) 'Come on, gie's your crack. Did ye hear. what happened to Pete? Fell aff his bike an' hurt his leg. Maister Will had to pick him up an' hurl him hame. A'weel, it's often happened the ither way roond . . . '

It was no use embarking on *my* story, so I sat and listened to Aggie's version. Then she asked, 'An' hoo's Jessie?'

My heart gave a lift even at the mention of Jessie's name. I knew the two had been in a 'place' together in their young days in a big house where one was a parlour-maid and the other a tablemaid, I think, though I never knew the distinction, or which was which; but they had been good friends.

'Tell her I was askin' for her.'

'Oh yes, I will, Aggie.'

A reminiscent look came into Aggie's eyes. 'The laughs we had!' said she, beginning to shake with laughter at the recollection.

'Mercy me!' I suddenly saw a new Jessie. Laughing!

'Ay, she was a great lass, Jessie. The lads were a' after her like a swarm o' bummy-bees.'

This time I was speechless.

'Thoosands o' them,' said Aggie lavishly. 'You ask her aboot Andy.'

'Andy?'

'Ay, he was the ane!'

'What about him, Aggie?'

'I'm no' tellin', said Aggie with a look of having gone too far.

Certainly she had whetted my appetite and given me food for thought for many a long day to come. Jessie laughing and larking with the lads!

'Here, wait!' said Aggie, suddenly shaking down her skirt and rising from her seat. She went through into her little bedroom and I heard her opening and shutting drawers. When she came back there were two faded photographs in her hand. This was better than the family album in the drawing-room. Brother William on his first pony, a long-ago Sunday School picnic, the whole family pictured outside the front door, a fierce-looking photograph of brother William in rugby-kit.

'Let me see, Aggie! Let me see!' I almost snatched them out of her hand, but she put one of them carefully in her skirt pocket before showing me the first. A picture of herself and Jessie in caps and aprons, their arms entwined, staring at the camera with giggly-looking smiles on their faces.

I hardly looked at Aggie. It was Jessie, the young Jessie, I wanted to see. Oh yes, that was my Jessie all right. How handsome she was. Not pretty, but something better. Dark hair with a crinkle in it, black flashing eyes, and a gypsyish look about her. But it was the smile that transformed her. I could almost swear as I peered closer at the picture that there was a dimple in her cheeks. Jessie! I could not help it. There was a lump in my throat. In another moment I would be 'bubblin' an' greetin'.'

I swallowed hard and said, 'Show me the other one, Aggie,' but while she was still fumbling for it the bell rang. Drawing-room. There was a row of them all marked. Dining-room, parlour, drawing-room, best bedroom. Aggie hastily put on her apron.

'I'll awa' an' see what the gentry want. Push the kettle nearer the fire, lassie, in case the teapot needs refilled.'

I sat there on the rug, thinking and wondering. How little one really knows of other folk. If it came to that, nobody knew *me*. But Jessie! How many more revelations were to come?

'Show me the other photo,' I begged Aggie when she came back carrying the tea-tray.

But Aggie, it seemed, had had second thoughts somewhere along the dark passage to the drawing-room.

'No, I'll no'. I daurna. Jessie wad kill me. Ye'd better

gang, lassie. They're for off.' She hauled me up from the rug. 'I tell ye what, you ask Jessie yoursel' aboot Andy.'

Would I ever dare?

The bell rang again; the signal that I had to go.

I threw my arms around Aggie and kissed her. I could never have done *that* with Jessie. But though Aggie was softer and more approachable, I knew for certain that I liked Jessie better.

There were only a few days left of the 'holiday'. The change of air, though it was only such a short distance away, had been intended to do us all good, and particularly to set Mother up for the birth of the baby later on in the year. Instead, it had been a disaster. We all looked worse. Peaky, short-tempered, and as for me I had caught 'beasts' in my hair. They had to be combed out with a small-tooth comb soaked in paraffin, a painful and degrading operation. I longed to be bald like Jock-the-herd.

Under Mother's supervision the farmhouse had begun to look a little tidier, but it was only on the surface. It would revert to a pigsty as soon as we were out of sight. I had a feeling, too, having overheard some whispered conversations between my parents, that the long-overdue chop was to come, if Father could brace himself sufficiently to administer it.

It would hurt him more than the easy-osy grieve, and I jaloused that when the time came he would dip his hand deep into his pocket to soften the blow and tide the fushionless family over their troubles.

But at least I had culled something out of that bleak holiday, if nothing else a collection of the 'thtorieth' I had made up to amuse Elsie and the rest of the brood. About Willy Weasel, Sandy Squirrel, Tommy Thrush, and wee Mary McFairy who had tartan wings and spoke with a lisp. They were to become the nucleus later on of tales broadcast in Children's Hour.

13. Crisis!

Home again!

Oh! it was great to turn in at our own roadend and rattle up the bumpy track past the cottages. Yes! there was Mrs Thing at the door shaking her rag rug, and her neighbour down on her hunkers pipe-claying the doorstep. We waved to them and they waved to us, not as if they were saluting the gentry. Far from it.

'That's them hame.'

We were just them.

Now we were in sight of the farmhouse. It was exactly the same as when we had left it – what else did I expect? – with smoke belching cheerfully from the kitchen chimney and the garden a tangle of flowers and weeds. Even the nettles looked nice.

The sun which had been missing all the time we were away shone out to welcome us home, but I did not need it to make my spirits soar. The very sight of Blackie sitting on the kitchen wall and the bubblyjock chasing a banty across the yard made me want to break into song. Polly Wolly Doodle! Anything would do.

My high spirits took a downward plunge when I discovered Jessie was not in the kitchen. Only the Cairthorse clattering about in her clogs.

'She's roond at the wesh-hoose.'

Jessie had left her mark on the kitchen table to welcome us home: a freshly baked batch of toddies, fadges and dropscones. There was a savoury smell from one of the pots by the fire. Stovies.

A picture-postcard lay on the table addressed to me, with a foreign stamp on it, the first I had ever received from Abroad. The ewe-lamb had written it in French, more or less, using the few phrases she had learned from Miss Crichton.

'*Comment allez-vous?*' As if she cared! '*Je suis bon. Le soleil est chaud ici. Beaucoup d'aventures. Je suis* enjoying *moimême . . .*'

I put it aside to study later, once I had seen Jessie. My first priority. Before dashing round to the wash-house I had a word with the Cairthorse.

'How are you, Liz-Ann?'

'No' bad.'

It was as much as I expected from the Cairthorse who would never admit to being jacko, like Aggie.

'Has anything been happening while we've been away?'

'Nut a thing.'

But she would have said that if the house had been burned down and the herd eaten by cannibals. It was only when her lad, George, was mentioned that Liz-Ann showed a glimmer of animation. I always thought of him as Gorge, which was how she spelled his name in the few painfully composed letters I had helped her to write, usually making an assignation at the crossroads.

George, as far as I knew, never wrote to her, but they had an understanding, and Liz-Ann had started sewing for her bottom drawer. A teacloth embroidered with clumsy lazy-daisy stitches, and a goonie, with lace round the edges, that would have fitted a baby elephant.

'I'm away round to the wash-house,' I told her.

'Uh-huh! Awa' ye go.'

There was something in the way she said it that made me take a closer look at the Cairthorse. She turned her face away but not before I noticed that her eyes were red and she appeared to be snivelling. Was it only one of her sniffy colds or had something dreadful happened to her lad?

'How's George?' I asked her.

'No' bad.'

'Have you seen him, Liz-Ann?'

'No, I've nut. I've no' been off.'

'But you'll be off tomorrow. Will you be meeting him then?'

'I might.'

Only might!

The snivel became more pronounced. It was not just a cold. Then suddenly she turned about and faced me.

'Jessie thinks I'm daft,' she burst out. (Well! we all thought *that*. Nobody could deny.) But there was more to it. 'She says I'm aff ma heid gaun wi' a lad like George.'

'Why?'

'She says there's naethin' in him.' Liz-Ann gulped. 'She ca'd him a spindly wee runt, an' she says naebody else wad look at him twice.' Liz-Ann echoed Jessie's words as if she were repeating the catechism. 'She says I should hae mair sense than rin efter the likes o' him. It'll never come to naethin'. He's no' worth a hait.' A hait being a minute particle.

'He is so!' I cried out, thinking of the lazy-daisy stitches and the voluminous nightgown. The poor creature looked so miserable that I longed to give her some grain of comfort. 'George is all right. He's nice.' I laid it on a bit thick. 'Ever so nice!'

I had only seen George once at the crossroads, pushing his bicycle and walking more or less beside the Cairthorse, together and yet not together, not looking or speaking to each other. Right enough, he was undersized and plain as porridge, but Liz-Ann was no raving beauty herself, and if they were fond of each other what did it matter? I thought of Mr Smith, the science master, with his wispy hair and bulging waistcoat. He was no Sir Galahad, yet how willingly I would have met *him* at the crossroads.

For the first time in my life I felt my birse rising against Jessie. She was wrong. Instinctively, I knew it; and though I felt a traitor, talking against her behind her back, I said so flat out.

'She's wrong! Don't you listen to Jessie, Liz-Ann. It's your business. It has nothing to do with her. Never heed what she says. George is all right. He's better . . .' Better than nothing, I was going to say, but stopped myself in time.

The Cairthorse began to knuckle away her tears as I continued with my advice. 'Just you go and meet him tomorrow. You will, won't you, Liz-Ann?'

'Ay, I wull.'

She gave a great sigh and stopped snivelling. Good for me, I thought! At the same time I felt guilty about Jessie.

'She'll likely be needin' mair sape,' said the Cairthorse, handing me a large bar of carbolic. 'Will ye tak' it roond to her?'

I took the soap and rushed away round to the wash-house, forgetting everything except the joyful prospect of seeing her again. Jessie! Jessie!

There she was, my anchor in life, the same yesterday, today and forever. No hugs or kisses, though I longed to throw myself into her arms. A look was enough. At least she gave me that; a long steady look that said everything, and then she went on with her work.

She was possing the clothes in a big tub, thumping the dirt out of them with a woden poss-stick as if she was giving them their licks. 'Take that! And that!'

She had been using the scrubbing-board, too. I could see that her hands were soft and wrinkled from immersion in soapy water. Nearby some sheets were boiling and bubbling in a pot which spilled over now and again, sending trickles of hot suds along the floor.

The wash-house was only a shed in the steading which the hinds used for odd jobs during wet weather. The turnip-cutter stood in one corner and the cross-cut saw in another beside Jessie's mangle. Sometimes the men came here to make straw ropes, but not if Jessie was in residence. Today it was her domain.

Having recovered from the first upsurge of pleasure at seeing her again, I stood back to take a closer look at her, trying to recapture the young Jessie I had seen in the faded photo. Yes, she was there all right, the same in essence, though her hair was steel grey and the soft look had given way to one of rigid repression. What matter that her cheeks were no longer smooth? I knew and loved every wrinkle in her face.

'What are ye glowerin' at, wumman?' she said, aware of my stare.

'I'm just looking.'

'A'weel, hand me the sape.'

She went on possing, while I stood there in one of my half-dwams, pondering on what might have happened if she had married her Andy, and why she hadn't. Maybe someone had turned *her* against him, as she had tried to do with the Cairthorse.

'It's God's will,' she often said, all planned from above.

'Nonsense!' I cried out, emerging from my dwam and suddenly realising it was not God who made a mess of folk's lives. It was folk themselves. Even splendid folk like Jessie.

At that moment I saw the light, and my life was changed for ever.

The wash-house was my Road to Damascus.

That moment of re-birth is so firmly etched in my mind that I have only to smell soapy-suds and I am back there hearing the thud-thud of the poss-stick and the bubbling of the boiler. A hen who had been cackling in the corner came half-running, half-flying past me on her way out to the yard, exuberant after delivering her egg.

Not as exuberant as I, suddenly relieved of a thousand chains that had been binding me, stultifying my young life till I was not myself but merely a pale shadow of everyone around me, especially anyone in authority. But from now on it would be different.

I would be *me*.

There is a time for everything, the Good Book tells us. This was my time. Why it should have happened now I had no idea. It must have been building up inside me for long enough, brought to a head perhaps by the dreary holiday at Swinside and by poor snivelling Liz-Ann.

It was not just that, it was everything in the past, all the times I had been put down by my superiors and made to feel inadequate. A daft bairn with no rummlegumption. Suddenly in a split-second I saw myself inside-out. Flyped, as Jessie was flyping one of Father's shirts before shoving it into the tub; and inside I was no worse than anyone else. No better, maybe; but as good as. Why had I never thought of it before? There was no time now to think it out properly, to pull the thread through the needle. I would have to go away by myself, straighten it out and tie a knot at the end; but the difficult part was over. I had found the needle and inserted the thread through the eye.

Meantime I tried to put my new-found confidence into practice.

'Jessie!'

'Ay, what?'

I took the plunge.

'He can't help being a spindly wee runt,' I burst out. It was not the Cairthorse I was defending as much as trying to pit myself against authority.

'What are ye bletherin' aboot?' said Jessie, not taking much notice of me.

'George.'

'Whae?'

Jessie gave me one of her looks but I stood my ground. 'Liz-Ann's lad.'

'Her!'

'Yes, her!' I said defiantly. 'She's a human being.'

'She's a human disaster. D'ye ken what she did the ither day? Spilt a hale pail-fou o' milk on the clean kitchen flair, an' she's broken the back-kitchen windy an' an ashet, forbye.'

'No point in breaking her heart, too.'

Jessie paused in her possing to take a closer look at me.

'What's up wi' ye, ye silly lassie? Are ye no' feelin' richt?'

'I'm feeling fine.' Never felt better!

'A'weel, ye're no' lookin' it,' declared Jessie. 'Ye're peely-wallier than ever. A dose o' castor-ile's what ye're needin'.'

I knew I was not tackling this in the right way, but I persisted. Tackle it I must.

'Jessie! what if it had been you?' You and Andy, I wanted to say, but I could not go as far as that.

'Me?'

'If it had been you and George.'

'Him!' She blew the lather from her hands – the graith – and continued, 'I'd hae mair sense than look the road *he's* on, a shilpit wee cratur like thon.'

'But what if he had been somebody else? Somebody you liked?'

She wiped her hands on her rough brat and said impatiently, 'I've got nae time for riddles. What's got into ye, lassie? Is the black dog on your back?'

'No, Jessie.' I urged myself to go on and make my point, however feebly. 'I'm just sticking up for Liz-Ann, and for myself. I've got as much right to an opinion as anyone else.'

'Maybe ay an' maybe hooch-ay!'

'Big folk are not always right,' said I, bracing myself. 'You're sometimes wrong, Jessie! Me, too, of course,' I conceded, 'but not all the time. So from now on I'm going to make up my own mid.' As a parting shot I added, 'And you can keep your castor-oil!'

She was at the scrubbing-board now, rubbing for dear life as if scrubbing out all my sins. She whipped round for a second. Was she going to give me a clout on the ear? I felt the colour rushing to my cheeks in anticipation of the blow, but she held her hand.

In that brief second during which our eyes met I tried to tell her everything I was feeling. I could not say the words right out.

'Jessie, I love you! You are my shield and strength, from whence cometh mine aid. But you are you, and I am me. The time has come for me to loosen the chains and go on in my own way, so that I can find out who I am. Always looking back in gratitude to you for setting me on the straight road. Do you understand, Jessie?'

I wonder if she did? There was just a flicker in her dark eyes as they met mine. Then she turned back to the scrubbing-board and said, 'Get oot ma road. It's high time ye lairnt some rummlegumption.'

'I've learnt it, Jessie,' I said, and ran off to my castle on the hill to think it all out.

14. A Fresh Beginning?

I could see father in the greenhouse perched on an up-turned pail, playing the jew's harp. He, too, had retired into his shell in search of solitude.

I climbed the crumbling walls of the old keep, moss-covered and with ferns growing from the crannies. I sat there for a long time looking towards the Carter Bar, not seeing the hills or anything around me, stunned by what had happened to me.

I sensed that I had passed a milestone. Gained something; lost something, too. I could no longer take the easy way out, merge into the background, believe everything I was told. Bairns should be seen and not heard. Life would be more difficult now; more exciting, perhaps. But I would still need Jessie as an anchor. Maybe more than ever now; but on different terms.

I came to no great conclusions with all my thinking, except that I knew I had found myself. Was I worth finding?

A skylark singing overhead echoed my feelings. 'Free! Free!'

Flora, the white pony, came galloping by, nickering with joy at being alive. Things had changed for her, too. since the motor had taken her place. Did she regret losing her chains? She lay down on the grass and rolled over and over, kicking up her heels. 'Free! Free!'

A bright butterfly settled on the castle wall beside me. It reminded me of a poem Miss Paleface, the English teacher, had read to us at the Grammar School. She had a book called an Anthology out of which she read now and again at the end of a lesson, picking the poems at random. I think she liked hearing the sound of her genteel voice, but it was the poems I liked.

> The tulip and the butterfly
> Appear in gayer coats than I.
> Let me be dressed fine as I will,
> Flies, worms, and flowers exceed me still.

So who was I to be thinking so much about myself? A mere article, as Jessie would have said; but an article with new-found faith in herself. I'll show them! I'll do something with my life! You wait!

'Man-lassie, ye'll tummle doon, if ye dinna watch oot.'

Jock-the-herd had come stravaiging across the hill with Jed and Jess at his heels. He was leaning on his crook, *his* strength in time of need, while the dogs lay panting on the grass. The herd blended into the background, as if he were part of the Cheviots himself.

'Hullo, Jock.'

'Ye're back.'

'Ay, I'm back, Jock.' But I'm a different me. Do you not notice the change? Not him! Perhaps if I had turned into a black-faced yowe he might.

Jock never wasted words, so I thought that was the end of the conversation, but I was surprised when he spoke again, and almost fell off the castle wall when I heard what he had to say.

'She'll be pleased to see ye back.'

'Who, Jock?'

'Jessie, of course. She's missed ye. She's been doon in the plook.' Down in the mouth, he meant.

I was astounded, not only at the thought of Jessie being doon in the plook because of me, but at the herd noticing it. When he and Jessie met face-to-face in the farmyard they never even acknowledged each other's presence.

There was more to everyone than met the eye.

The skylark was still singing overhead and I wanted to sing with it, elated to know that Jessie had missed me and that my feelings for her were not just one-sided.

I wished the herd would go on, but he had reverted to normal and was as dumb as a drystane dyke till we heard a tinny bell ringing from the distance. The dinner-bell calling me home. Sometimes I took note of it, if it came up my back, or if I was hungry.

I felt hungry now. Toom in the waim. I could almost smell the stovies. So I slithered down from the castle wall, dislodging a stone or two, and ran away home, forgetting all my introspective thoughts. I was only a starving bairn in need of sustenance.

Jessie was dishing the meal when I came in. The castor-oil bottle stood on the table beside my plate, but I took no notice of it. I knew, and I think Jessie knew, too, it was only there as a gesture. The cork would not come out.

She did not look at me but ladled a helping on to my plate.

'Eat up your stovies, lassie,' she said in her usual sharp tone.

'Yes, Jessie, I will. They smell good.' My tone was warmer.

Her hand lingered near my cheek. Was she going to

touch it? Give me an unexpected little pat perhaps? No! she changed her mind and gave me a slap instead. A wee skelp.

It stung for a moment, but it was almost as good as a caress.

Other Arrow Books of interest:

A BREATH OF BORDER AIR

Lavinia Derwent

'Looking back, I often wonder if any of it was real . . .'

Lavinia Derwent, well known as a best-selling author of children's books and as a television personality, here memorably portrays a childhood spent on a lonely farm in the Scottish Border country.

Here was an enchanted world of adventure: a world of wayward but endearing farm animals, and of local characters like Jock-the-herd . . . and Lavinia's closest friend, Jessie, who never failed to temper her earthy wisdom with a rare sense of humour.

'Any exiled Scot will breathe this fine air with joy' *Yorkshire Post*

THE HILLS IS LONELY

Lillian Beckwith

When Lillian Beckwith advertised for a quiet, secluded place in the country, she received the following unorthodox description of the attractions of life on an isolated Hebridean croft:

'Surely it's that quiet here even the sheeps themselves on the hills is lonely and as to the sea it's that near I use it myself every day for the refusals . . .'

Intrigued by her would-be landlady's letter and spurred on by the sceptism of her friends, Lillian Beckwith replied in the affirmative THE HILLS IS LONELY is the hilarious and enchanting story of the extremely unusual rest cure that followed.

BESTSELLING FICTION FROM ARROW

All these books are available from your bookshop or news-agent or you can order them direct. Just tick the titles you want and complete the form below.

☐	THE COMPANY OF SAINTS	Evelyn Anthony	£1.95
☐	HESTER DARK	Emma Blair	£1.95
☐	1985	Anthony Burgess	£1.75
☐	2001: A SPACE ODYSSEY	Arthur C. Clarke	£1.75
☐	NILE	Laurie Devine	£2.75
☐	THE BILLION DOLLAR KILLING	Paul Erdman	£1.75
☐	THE YEAR OF THE FRENCH	Thomas Flanagan	£2.50
☐	LISA LOGAN	Marie Joseph	£1.95
☐	SCORPION	Andrew Kaplan	£2.50
☐	SUCCESS TO THE BRAVE	Alexander Kent	£1.95
☐	STRUMPET CITY	James Plunkett	£2.95
☐	FAMILY CHORUS	Claire Rayner	£2.50
☐	BADGE OF GLORY	Douglas Reeman	£1.95
☐	THE KILLING DOLL	Ruth Rendell	£1.95
☐	SCENT OF FEAR	Margaret Yorke	£1.75

Postage _____

Total _____

ARROW BOOKS, BOOKSERVICE BY POST, PO BOX 29, DOUGLAS, ISLE OF MAN, BRITISH ISLES

Please enclose a cheque or postal order made out to Arrow Books Limited for the amount due including 15p per book for postage and packing both for orders within the UK and for overseas orders.

Please print clearly

NAME..

ADDRESS..

....

Whilst every effort is made to keep prices down and to keep popular books in print, Arrow Books cannot guarantee that prices will be the same as those advertised here or that the books will be available.